THOUGHTS
ON
KARATE

By
Les Bubka

Dedication

To my teachers; past, present and future.

Acknowledgments

This book would not have been possible without the help and encouragement of many people; I would like to express my gratitude to those that helped the most.

Firstly, I would like to thank my wife, Anna, for her patience and encouragement as well as for picking on my grammar. I would like to thank John Titchen for checking the content and offering valuable advice. I would also like to thank Chris Hanson for reading my draft manuscript and for providing kind words for the foreword alongside that of John Titchen's.

Last but not least, a big thanks to my students and friends for their support!

Foreword

Consistency is the defence of a small mind.

Humans are inconsistent. They should be. An individual that does not change any of their views over time is one that has not grown. Experience and exposure to new ideas, experiences and people should inform our approaches and engender change. The openness and ability to adapt and change is a strength; recognising when, what and how to change is wisdom.

Written between 2014 and 2020 these thoughts reflect Les Bubka's ever growing and changing insights on the Karate he teaches and trains and on the potential of the art as a whole. The diverse subjects chart not only Les' journey as a Karateka but also his development as a writer, expressing himself with ever greater clarity in a second language. From safe physical training to mental health, these eclectic articles are thought provoking and may challenge the preconceptions of many about how they approach their own discipline. Les does not ask or expect that you think along the same lines as him on every topic, but he does ask that you think.

You could sit and read this book cover to cover, but perhaps greater benefit would be gained from dipping into it regularly for insights and inspiration. Thoughts on Karate has value for both beginners and more experienced readers, and just as Les has changed over the course of writing this book so readers may find that the same chapters take on different meanings if they revisit them at different points in their own martial journey.

John Titchen
Author and leading exponent of the practical application of Karate
www.titchen.com

****

I founded Karate Unity (www.karateunity.ca, on Instagram, YouTube, and Facebook) for the purpose of uniting like-minded martial artists and combat sport players globally. After 35+ years of training in several Okinawan Karate styles and combat sports, I felt it was time to create a platform to share my expression of Karate, along with my cross-training discoveries into other arts and combat sports. My conclusions, to date, has been that as long as we are human, no matter what we study, we will move in similar ways as martial artists, we will seek similar ways to protect ourselves, and we will call these techniques different things based on culture, context, and individual need.

Karate Unity has allowed me to meet phenomenal martial artists such as Sensei Les Bubka. I met Les on Facebook several years ago where we shared our common passions: Karate and Combat Sports. Social media and modern technology have allowed us to communicate through direct messaging and video conferencing. I have enjoyed all of our time together discussing martial arts techniques, philosophies, and concepts. I met Les for the first time when he attended one of my UK Karate Unity Seminars in High Wycombe, July 2019. He was my Uke for one of my demonstrations, and I experienced first-hand how he seamlessly integrates Wrestling into his Karate. As part of a trapping response drill that I showed, Les quickly closed the distance, shot a duck-under and threw me. It was quite amazing to have met him finally, and most importantly, to experience his high level of martial arts abilities. His versatility in several Martial Arts and Combat Sports, along with his open mindedness, and kind heartedness permeates throughout his new book, Thoughts on Karate.

Thoughts on Karate is a collection of articles, essays, and reflections which elucidates and encompasses who Les truly is as a person and Martial Artist. Master Gichin Funakoshi once said *"The ultimate aim of Karate lies not in victory nor defeat, but in the perfection of the character of its participants"*. I feel that this sentiment is clearly found in several of Les' articles. In the articles Care About Others, along with, Honor and Diligence, Les discusses how we as martial artists need to remove our ego from our practice, and treat each other with kindness and respect both inside and outside of the dojo. This clearly shows how positive character development supersedes physical prowess. Furthermore, Les selflessly shares his knowledge and his time with people having unique needs and exceptionalities. Karate for Mental Health, for example, is an initiative that Les has spear-headed in the UK, and continues to manage year after year, bringing Karate to those who need it in order to manage their life with stressful mental conditions. I am both honored and grateful to have been associated with a gentleman who continually gives back to the world community.

In his book, the article Kata to Fighting, is one that I connected to dearly. I smiled when I read that he teaches beginners the principles behind fighting alongside with the applications. He also engages his students in progressive resistance drills with equipment in a cross-training environment. This is synonymous with my own practice along with what I teach to my students. I firmly believe this is an extremely healthy way to develop students as they can clearly see why they are doing what they are doing, along with discovering what works and what doesn't work through sparring. Finally, the article Kano Paradox – Art vs. Sport, is one that I connected to the most. Les stated, *"As I am doing both an art and a sport, I have views from both sides and like to mix all the benefits and concepts from sports and traditional martial arts."* This, to me, spoke to me the most. I believe in the marriage of all arts and combat sports together. All martial arts and combat sports have something to offer. Once you recognize the context and what you need it for, you should study it and integrate it inside of your game. Les is a perfect specimen of this. After training with him personally, I clearly see how he integrates all ranges of combat into his practice through his exposure to striking and grappling arts and sports.

When reading Thoughts on Karate allow yourself to reflect, compare, and think about your own Martial Arts practice from a similarities and differences perspective. I enjoyed reading Les' book from the lens of a friend and fellow martial artist; it has confirmed every positive thing I know about the man and his Karate practice.

I wish you all a thoughtful reading experience! Enjoy.

Chris Hanson
Martial Arts Instructor,
Founder of Karate Unity www.karateunity.ca
Toronto, Ontario

Contents

Chapter 1 - Introduction

Moving to the UK was stressful for me. Aside from the general upheaval of moving from one country to another, my English was far from perfect and it turned out that I had in fact learnt American English which made communication even harder.

After deciding to stay in the UK I thought it would be a good idea to try and improve my language skills. I asked my co-workers, friends, and anyone that I came across to correct me. This was particularly challenging with some people as their approach went along the lines of *"I know what you mean, so don't worry about it."*. I did not want to just be understood, I wanted to be able to say what I meant in a more elaborate way than *"Les eat. Les drink."* etc.

My next step was to watch TV with the subtitles on. This was great as it improved my spelling and grammar, but it did cause an interesting problem. I would catch and remember the odd word here and there, generally ones that sounded cool in my head. However, this created a slightly bizarre, multi-accent mixture of words. Some would sound Scottish, others Welsh, but mostly I was speaking English with a harsh Polish accent. This made me very difficult to understand for some people.

Fast forward eight years and I had started to speak

fluently and understand most of the people that I met. The next stage for me was to improve my writing skills. So, I started to write a blog called 'Something like that' which took its name from a phrase that my friends had noticed I often used when teaching martial arts (this has subsequently evolved into my Les Bubka Karate Jutsu blog). Luckily my wife is both highly educated and English, so with her help I was able to post articles on my blog in well written English. But the process of putting together a blog was a bit longer than just writing an article. I started out with an idea. Then I would write an article myself, trying to construct it as grammatically correct as I could. Anna would then read this first attempt, marking the mistakes and re-writing it with me so that I could understand how I should have written it. This helped me to improve my English immensely.

My learning is far from complete and the more I write, the more I learn. This process of trying to improve my English has led me to become an unexpected author.

This book represents a collection of articles that I have written over the years and should show the evolution of my writing as well as how my thoughts on Karate have changed over time.

For a while now my friends and those who have attended my seminars or come across my Karate have asked me to write down the technical aspects of Shin Ai Do, its methodology and concepts. Most of them have never heard of Shin Ai Do Karate, which is understandable as it is now practically a non-existent system. I believe that I am one of only a handful of active teachers left. I have thought about capturing the essence of this style on paper before and have actually started to compose a book a few times, but every time I start, I get stuck because of one thing, the only thing that is constant in life – change. As I have developed in Karate my version of Shin Ai Do has developed too and this work is not finished yet. Every time I meet people who influence me I adapt / modify aspects in my Karate.

To be honest I am a very different Karateka now than I was when I started training in Shin Ai Do in the late 90s, but I respect my roots and feel a strong attachment to the style that has moulded me. Many times I had thought to move away from Karate (for example to MMA or Kickboxing), but Karate is in my heart, my soul and my mind. It fits perfectly in my opinion the way that I think about martial arts.

I am not ready to write the Shin Ai Do book just yet, but can instead offer you some insight on the evolutionary process of my way of the empty hand. This process covers aspects from techniques, organisation, methodology to philosophy. Hopefully my path and logic will be apparent although I admit at times it might be confusing as I have always been drawn to the chaotic side of evolution!

For some articles I have added some afternotes that represent my revised thoughts on the subject based on my knowledge now. For example, if I have subsequently changed my opinion or have since learned that I was wrong.   In these cases, I have kept the original article text to provide an indication of my development.

I hope that you enjoy these articles and am very grateful for your support.

Chapter 2 - About this Book

For ease of reading I have grouped my articles into three categories that are detailed in the following chapters. I hope that this will make navigation more logical and friendly. These categories reflect my opinions on:

- General Training
- Philosophy
- Techniques

I hope that this collection will be enjoyable to read and thought provoking. These are my own thoughts, comments and opinions, they might differ to your own.

Chapter 3 - General Training

In this chapter I focus on my personal journey in Karate, how I teach, and what the structure of my club is like. I examine teaching methodologies, outcomes and procedures. I also dive into the benefits of Karate, the projects that I am engaged in and I express my personal opinions / observations about the problems that Karate as an art is facing.

Shin Ai Do Introduction and Concepts

12th of July 2014

In this article I would like to say a few things about our Karate style, Shin Ai Do. I have been prompted to write this article thanks to a question from one of my blog readers, Alex. His question made me realise that perhaps I should explain a little bit more about our club and the history of our style. I hope you will enjoy it.

What is Shin Ai Do?

Shin Ai Do Karate is a modern Karate style that inherits from traditional Karate schools such as Goju Ryu and Kyokushin. The name Shin Ai Do was first used in

6

1989 to describe a school of Karate developed in Russia.

Figure 1 - Shin Ai Do Karate Logo

Our logo comprises an outer circle, known as Enso in Japanese, and the Kanji for Shin Ai Do. Enso is a Japanese word signifying a circle and has no single, fixed meaning. A popular expression in Zen painting, it symbolizes a moment when the mind is free enough to simply let the body or spirit create. The brushed ink of the circle shows the expressive movement of the spirit in time. The Enso circle also symbolizes strength, enlightenment, harmony, elegance, and the universe. The term "Shin Ai Do" means "Way of True Harmony", which echoes the principle aims of the style. These are for a practitioner to execute techniques in a flowing manner that is in harmony with the advances of an attacker, and more broadly, for a practitioner to find a style of fighting that is in harmony with their own abilities. As well as being interpreted as "Shin Ai Do" our Kanji can also be read as "Makoto Ai Michi", which means "Sincere Teaching". This also represents our way of training in that there is not an emphasis on making money from our students.

The main distinction between Shin Ai Do and some other styles of Karate is that Shin Ai Do training focusses on adopting a way of thinking as opposed to just learning a particular set of techniques by rote.

Components of Shin Ai Do

Shin Ai Do uses strikes, throws, sweeps and ground fighting techniques that support fighting against an opponent in a variety of scenarios. In all cases the aim is to use an attacker's power against himself/herself.

We strongly emphasise safety in our club for our students and so we use head guards and small gloves with a variety of other standard protective equipment such as shin pads, groin protectors, gum shields etc. Using these safety measures we are able to simulate realistic fighting, but in a relatively safe environment.

A few words about me

My name is Les Bubka and I am the instructor at Guildford Shin Ai Do. I originally started training in Oyama Karate in 1992 in Krakow, Poland. In 1997 after a short break due to injury I was dragged by a friend of mine to begin training in Shin Ai Do Karate under Sensei

Artur Marchewka (a big thank you to my friend Piotr as switching to Shin Ai Do has changed my life!).

In 2002 I passed my instructor's exam and opened my first dojo in Krakow. Two years later I opened another two dojos in Proszowice and Koscielec and by 2003 my students were taking part in many competitions with great success. Training hard whilst working as a professional instructor, I successfully gained my 1st Dan in 2007 having completed my exam in front of an international commission from Idokan Europa and Idokan Europa Poland. After moving to the United Kingdom, I was lucky enough to have the opportunity to start the UK branch of Shin Ai Do in 2008. In 2009, at an international seminar in Krakow, I achieved my 2nd Dan. Currently, as I am writing this article, I am preparing for my 3rd dan grading in August.

Training Goals

Our students set their pace and priorities. If they want to train without testing, that is up to them. Most martial arts instructors will constantly assess the progress of their students. There are basically two paths trainee can choose when training with us.

- Rank and File – they want to continue the association path to black belt and above. Learn all the history, ceremonies and Japanese names etc.

- Just Train – Students just want to train and learn. They will not be expected to memorize the Japanese words and philosophies.

Shin Ai Do Functional Karate

In my opinion the main function of Karate is fighting. That is what we teach and therefore some of our kata performances are far from aesthetical perfection, but they work on a resisting opponent.

I hope that this short description of Shin Ai Do Karate will help in understanding my point of view.

Our vision of Functional Karate is not the only way, there are other great paths, but all the roads lead to the same mountain peak, whichever way we get there is not important.

I will mention one more thing which makes me stay with my teacher Sensei Artur and the very small school of Karate that he represents – Shin Ai Do. When I arrived for my first lesson Artur said very few words to me. He told me about his school and what I could expect, but also, he told me something very unexpected which I did not understand at first. He said *"After this class please visit a few of the other schools of martial arts around here and attend some lessons there so that you can choose the right school, the one best suited for you. One day I hope you will return and join our club".* And so I did after a few visits to other clubs... It is now my 17th year with Artur as my teacher. Through all these years he has always encouraged me to visit different martial arts and sports, to learn from them what I can. As a result of my Sensei's influence I am now training in Wrestling, Kempo and other systems.

Now that I am a teacher myself I try to encourage others to be open and to try to explore other possibilities as we never know what is just around the corner. It makes me proud when my students find the art, sport or hobby which makes them happy even if that means that they are leaving my dojo, I am happy for them. They all know (so I hope) that from the first time they step into my dojo they have entered the family of Shin Ai Do where they can get Sincere Teaching in the art of Karate.

- Afternote-

A lot has changed since this introduction was written over six years ago. My view on Karate has been altered dramatically. I still think that the primary function of Karate is as a fighting or self-protection system, but for me now I feel drawn towards its health benefits, both physical and mental. As a lot of us are lucky enough to live in a mostly benign environment I prefer to focus on training as an art with some self-protection skills rather than for pure self-defence. This is not to say that my way is the best way, everyone has to choose their own priorities.

As an aside I am also happy to say that I did in fact pass my 3rd dan examination that year and have subsequently gone on to obtain my 4th dan at an international seminar in July 2018.

Learning Model at Shin Ai Do

15th of April 2016

In life we constantly learn new skills. Starting from a young age we are introduced to different models of learning. In Karate just like in other subjects we have to have a structure of progression through the education levels.

In our Karate style we have a simple and transparent way of teaching students of any grade from beginner to advanced. This structure is based on the traditional model of teaching in martial arts.

Knowledge Passing Model
(from generation to generation, from master to student)

Figure 2- Knowledge Passing Model

Knowledge is passed from generation to generation, from master to student. In the dojo environment the teacher is the main source of knowledge.

Teaching Transmission
(from one Sensei to many students)

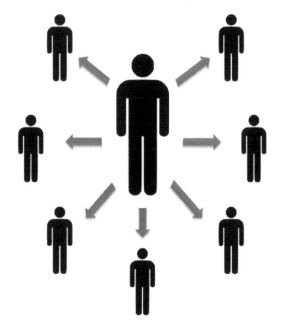

Figure 3 - Teaching Transmission

To understand the relationship between teachers and students we need to know the grade structure and terminology in use in the dojo environment.

Structure within the Organisation

師範   Shihan (5th Dan) = Professor / Master / Instructor

先生   Sensei (3rd Dan) = Teacher / Instructor

先輩   Sempai = Senior Student (based on grade)

後輩   Kohai = Junior Student (based on grade)

Figure 4 - Grade Structure

Now that we know who is who in the dojo let's take a look at how the knowledge is distributed throughout the organisation.

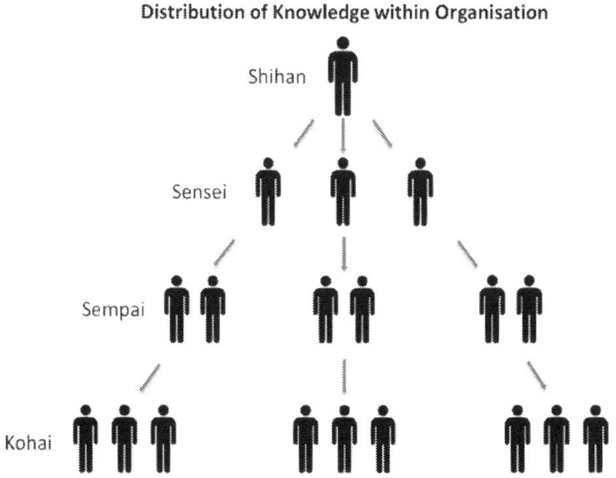

Distribution of Knowledge within Organisation

Figure 5 - Knowledge Distribution

Taking into consideration the time and effort it takes to achieve mastery in Karate there will always be more students than teachers. Passing knowledge via the traditional (Japanese) model differs from the modern (Western) model. In the modern model the Sensei passes knowledge to students who then focus on their own progress.

Western Learning Model

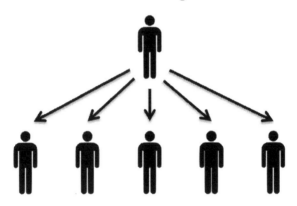

Figure 6 - Western Learning Model

In the traditional model students receive instructions from the Sensei and they have to pass this on to lower grade students, so the least experienced students get more information from more sources than in the modern model.

16

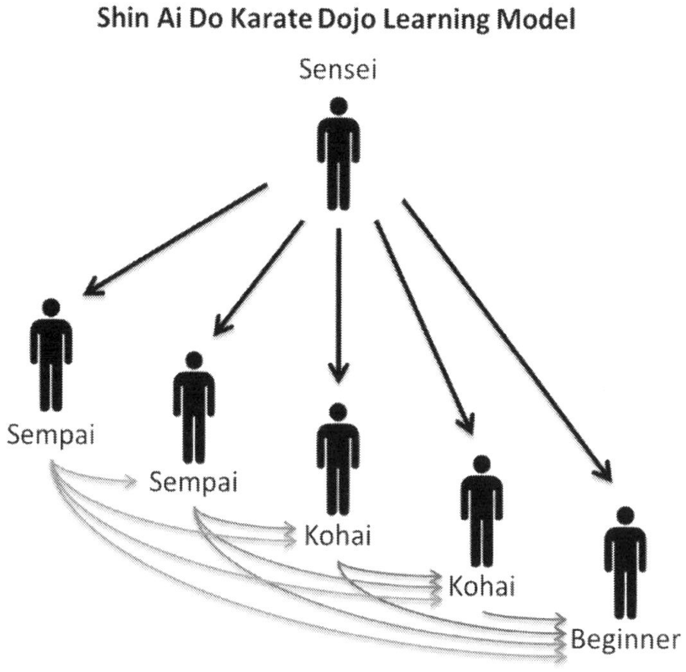

Shin Ai Do Karate Dojo Learning Model

Figure 7 - Shin Ai Do Karate Learning Model

There is another mechanism in place at our organisation that is different when compared to some others. A lot of western dojos have their Sensei focus most of their attention on beginners. This can lead to higher grades not learning anything new due to lack of support, which can result in them quitting.

Western Dojo – Model of Investment

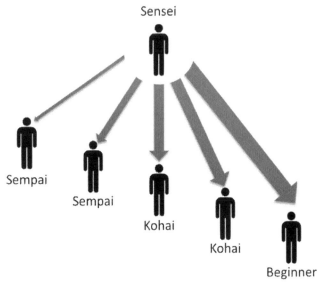

Figure 8 - Western Dojo - Model of Investment

For us, the highest graded students get the most attention and instruction to make sure that they are continuing to advance their knowledge.

Shin Ai Do – Model of Investment in Students

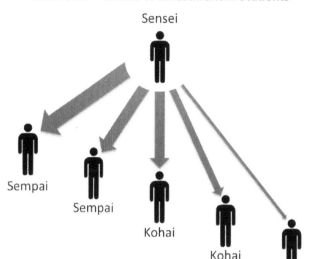

Figure 9 - Shin Ai Do Dojo - Model of Investment

It is not that the Kohai is left alone to blindly copy Sempais and Sensei, they do have some of their attention, but they mainly benefit from being facilitated by all of the higher grades.

Process of Knowledge Distribution in the Dojo

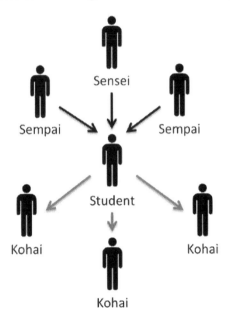

Figure 10 - Knowledge Distribution Process

In our club all of our students and teachers have responsibilities. The Sensei passes on knowledge and Sempais are absorbing and passing this knowledge on to the Kohais. With time and grade responsibility grows.

Level of Responsibility in the Dojo

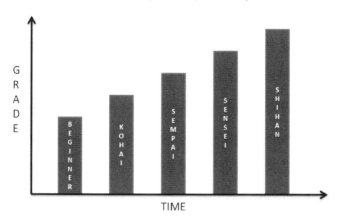

Figure 11 - Level of Responsibility in the Dojo

As an organisation there are two models of seeking knowledge – open and closed. The latter model means that students are restricted to only one source of knowledge, their own organisation. In Shin Ai Do we prefer and encourage an open model.

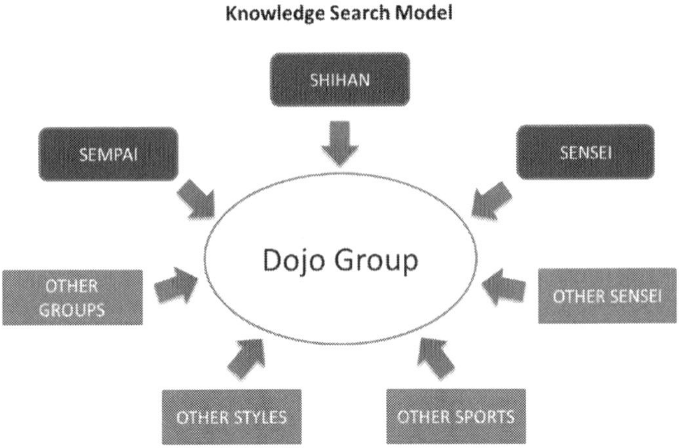

Knowledge Search Model

Figure 12 - Knowledge Search Model

We recommend to our members that they not only learn from other styles of Karate, but that they try to find useful information from other martial arts and sports.

I hope that this short article has managed to demonstrate our simple learning model.

Sinusoidal Karate

4th of April 2015

Sinusoidal Karate. What do I mean? All processes in life go like a sinusoid up, and down, so does my martial arts training, especially Karate. On the way to the mountain top we choose different paths some going up then going down, at one time we are in love with our art and then we fall out of love, just to find our passion again later.

For some time I have lost my passion for Karate and turned more attention to wrestling and boxing. It seems to be that my brain needs some rest from one thinking pattern and chooses to perform other tasks as a self-preservation technique. I have gone through this before a few times, interestingly it always comes back with more passion and a breakthrough. Then my Karate progresses and I can see obvious things which were just in front of me but not previously seen.

I think that this process allows me to step away and do other stuff then come back with a more open mind clear from previous ways. From the beginning I have tried to fight this and to keep myself motivated and interested in Karate but this was suffering. Then I discovered that actually letting go gives me more benefits and I am sure that Karate is faithful and always comes back to me without judging me.

It feels like Karate rewards me for coming back a bit

more humbled then when I left. A bit like the father who always take you back after an argument where you were sure you were right but after stepping away realised that you were wrong. That is the way life goes.

Now I think I am ready to step back in to this sea called Karate and explore it with a new approach. As I had time to get a hunger for Karate again some changes occurred in our club. Maybe it is my fault that the club went down in numbers, maybe it was meant to be. Now I am happy to train in a group of two but willing to do thoughtful, hard quality training, not dropping standards to satisfy other people's needs.

A lot of people think that Karate training should be physical and easy, you come for training and you are released from the responsibility of thinking just to perform patterns, mindless repetitions of kata and bunkai not getting anything from or putting anything into them. Well when I teach Karate I am expecting students to think, ask, challenge and try to prove me wrong. As a teacher I dream about my students being better than me, but to do that you have to think. The best example of this mindlessness is a story about tradition, told to me by one of my teachers - all of the students were making funny mouth expressions when performing kiba dachi (horse stance), everyone did it because their teacher had done it. When asked why they did this grimace? All answered because it was sticking to the tradition of their school and that their master does that. But none of the students asked their teacher why he is doing this, if they did they would know that he was suffering with haemorrhoids and this position was just uncomfortable for him.

What is the moral of this story? Quite simple; do ask questions. There is no worse approach to learning than mindless monkey see, monkey do.

Adapting Karate

16th of May 2019

Martial arts are often perceived as being a very athletic activity that is reserved for very fit and fully abled people, mostly men aged between 16 to 30 something. This seems to be where most clubs are focussing in terms of their potential client base. Within Karate there tends to be more of an emphasis on children and so the image of Karate has been distorted into being a martial art that is ineffective, but is a great pastime with awesome coordination and discipline building features. This weak image is far from true and luckily there is a growing movement of pragmatic martial artists who are promoting the practical application of this great art, of which I am happy to be a part. I am also a strong advocate of the benefits of Karate in improving not only physical health but also mental wellbeing and as such I organise seminars and classes for organisations helping people who suffer with ill mental health. Being involved in this type of application of Karate has led me to focus on inclusion and developing Karate as an art that is accessible for all students, no matter what their physical ability, age or struggles may be. Everyone is welcome in my dojo (place of training) and I can see that this approach is increasing in popularity as more and more dojos are incorporating changes to enable all students to participate. If we think that there are over 11 million people with a disability in the UK, this is a considerable proportion of the population that could be excluded from enjoying the benefits of Karate.

In my club we have two types of groups:

- **Practical** Karate where we train with contact; sparring and throwing is a usual part of a session.

- **Meditation** Karate where we focus on a softer approach and enjoy the benefits of Karate forms.

In both of these groups we place an emphasis on adapting the training programme to accommodate all kinds of students. Most of the exercises within Karate can be appropriately modified. It just takes some knowledge and imagination. By doing this we can achieve astonishing results, empowering students and giving them the confidence to take part in activities from which they are usually excluded. For example, when working with seniors I have modified our kata (forms) to take into consideration the fact that most of my clients experience problems with joint mobility, arthritis, balance and back pain. My programme is designed to remove stances that are not so kind on joints and includes additional movements that help to improve balance.

What is important is to focus on an individual's abilities and make appropriate modifications as we teach. A good example would be the kata, Naihanchi, where we have a movement that involves crossing our legs to step. People with poor balance struggle to complete this move and so we have a few options on how to make this easier. First, we can abandon the step altogether and instead put in place a side shuffle. A second option is to place a chair in front of the person, which can be used as a support. In this way we can allow them to keep exercising without being discouraged and in time they can build up their confidence to try the cross step.

Another simple modification is to exclude some parts of a workout or drill. Just a few weeks ago we had two students who had acquired minor injuries to the ankle and calf. As we were working on pad drills that involved punches and kicks they were struggling with the kicking element and from the perspective of a coach it was too risky to allow them to kick. My responsibility as an instructor is to make sure that we can avoid obtaining injuries and do not worsen any existing ones and so the logical answer is to modify the drill to leave out kicks for those individuals. Having watched many classes at different clubs I had come across the practice that pushes students to train through an injury with the mantra that *"it will make you stronger"*. In my experience this does not make you stronger and in fact is more likely to result in you having to take a longer break from training to enable recovery. At many clubs this mistake can be easily made, where a technique has been excluded for a particular individual, but the other students have not been made aware that the drill has been modified for that person and so the effected individual is pressurised by others to perform the whole drill.

An adaptation that I have found very useful is to modify sparring conditions to appropriately consider individuals. Some of my students are hard of hearing whilst others have mild autism and so I have changed the way that they are pressure tested. In consultation with the given student we come up with a plan for their involvement in sparring, from engaging in sparring but with no hitting to the head to doing forms on the side instead. It is also important that my other students take into consideration their partners' ability. For instance, after a few years of training an autistic student decided that he would like to try full sparring with punches and kicks to the head (with protective headgear). This was not a problem as all of the students were made aware that they need to control themselves and not punch 100%. In this way everyone can enjoy the same activity whilst remaining safe.

We all associate Karate with strict discipline, lines of students and a loud *"Osu!"* (Acknowledgement). This is a reflection of Japanese Karate. Okinawans have a more family-oriented approach that is much more relaxed and I was always drawn to this sort of club. Many instructors have disagreed with my approach whereby students can drink during a session and ask questions freely. However, having stuck to my beliefs and run my club in this relaxed way for a few years I can happily say that it has been beneficial to my students. They care about the club and each other and the process of learning is much faster, especially for the more age-advanced students. Put simply, without stress we can enjoy training and as we all know it is much easier to learn a subject if it is enjoyable.

A fundamental element when teaching anything is communication. If there is no communication then it is very hard to learn anything. That is why it is very important to establish a sufficient and individual connection with students, in order to communicate clearly. What do I mean by this? If we have a group of students with different abilities we have to consider how we can effectively communicate with each of them without losing detailed instructions. For example, in our club we have a student that is deaf and in order to know what I am saying she has to be able to see my face (for lip reading), so I make sure that she can see my face whenever I explain something. In addition to ensuring that students can 'hear' you, it is also important to appropriately adjust the language that we use to enable us to be understood. People with learning difficulties or non-native English speakers might struggle to understand certain words or phrases and so we need to adjust our speech so as to be clear. For instance, people with autism might take our metaphors literally and so misinterpret what has been said leading to misunderstandings and potential injuries.

The examples that I have discussed here represent only a small subset of the adaptations that we can use to make the sharing of Karate with others successful. We need a personal approach that considers the needs of each student in order to provide the best possible instruction in a safe and friendly environment. If these changes can be more widely incorporated into teaching methods then we will hopefully see more people from all walks of life taking up and enjoying Karate in the future. In our dojo we have a saying that *"strong and caring people are the pillars of society and Karate helps to cultivate them"*. If people are strong both mentally and physically they are much more willing to support others and so the practice of Karate does not just help the individual that trains, but also the whole community within which that individual is a part.

Injury Prevention

31st of May 2014

During classes the instructor/sensei is obliged to create a safe environment for members of the club. Most of us think that wearing protective gear is all that is required – we put on our head gear, gloves, shin pads and we feel safe. This is true to some extent, but safety is much more.

As teachers we have to explain to students the importance of body mechanics and anatomy. Knowledge of how our bodies are designed and how they work is a key element of healthy training. For example, knowing the structure of the elbow and its mechanics will prevent over extending it when punching. Similarly, when kicking it is better to not use the full motion of the knee dynamically as our muscles do not have time to react to prevent over extension, in this case our hips should be used to help extend our range of movement. These few examples of anatomical knowledge illustrate how this is important to promoting the safe practice of techniques by students.

An additional safety measure is ensuring that training is conducted in a controlled environment. To provide this as instructors we have a responsibility to pay attention to how students behave. For instance, observing their fighting manners, their egos and their approach to wearing safety equipment. If we notice that one of our fighters behaves dangerously when sparring or is rude it is up to the instructor to intervene and correct the student, as if no intervention is made this may result in injury.

Another danger at the dojo/gym is a person performing an exercise or drill without guidance and preparation. An example of this would be students being introduced to high throws without prior training of break falls. This is very dangerous and has in some unfortunate cases resulted in the death of the student being thrown.

On YouTube it is easy to find footage of completely unprepared people fighting and being beaten badly. I believe it is an instructor's responsibility to adequately prepare students to fight. For example I believe that it is irresponsible for an instructor to teach students light contact sparring when the instructor then sends them for full contact fights – these students will be ill prepared for the experience and are likely to get injured and/or shocked.

Consequently, when joining a dojo/club, I think it is always best to make sure that you check the qualifications of the instructor along with their insurance and consider whether the methods and equipment that they use during their sessions is as safe as reasonably practicable.

Training and the Immune System

18th of October 2014

This week I would like to have a closer look at the relationship between training and health. There is no doubt that engaging in regular physical activities improves our health. Exercising increases the production of white blood cells, which are responsible for our immune response to infections. In Poland we have a popular saying *"sport to zdrowie"*, in English *"sport is health"*; whilst this is true it is only true up to a certain point. When we increase the duration and intensity of our workouts, our immune system actually gets weaker.

A good study that supports this is one done by Dr David Nieman[1] who is a pioneer in the research area of exercise immunology at Appalachian State University. The study I refer to examined marathon runners at the Los Angeles Marathon in 1987. Dr Nieman himself took part in 58 marathons and noticed that when he ran around 144km a week he more often suffered from throat infections, however when he reduced this distance to below 100km the infections stopped. In examining the impact of marathon training on health Dr Nieman and his team questioned a randomly selected group of 4926 participants of the Los Angeles Marathon.

---

[1] Nieman, David & Johanssen, L & Lee, Jerry & Arabatzis, K. (1990). Infectious episodes in runners before and after the LA Marathon. The Journal of sports medicine and physical fitness. 30. 316-28.

The main interest of this study was history of infections before the marathon and health problems that occurred after the run. The study showed that for a long-distance runner the probability of getting an infection is nearly six times greater than people who run lesser distances. Dr Nieman suggests that athletes that run more than 100km a week double their risk of infection. It has been proven that this happens because training hard for long periods (over 1.5 hours) can weaken the immune system, with this effect lasting up to 24 hours. This study was published in the Journal of Applied Sciences in 2007.

Kancho Joko Ninomiya summarised this nicely by saying *"Don't train hard, train smart"*. In this way it is recognised that a *"good hard session"* in the dojo or gym is not always beneficial to our health. It is good sometimes to stop and think about our workout programmes to make sure that we are getting the best out of them.

Not All Roses

21st of November 2019

As most of you probably know I'm a strong advocate for the benefits of Karate in relation to mental health. As with everything in life there are two sides of the coin and rarely things are black and white.

For some individuals or groups Karate might have a negative impact on health both physically and mentally. Whether or not a person benefits positively from training depends on several factors such as:

- Personal circumstances
- Instructor
- Group social setup
- Training methods

Personal Circumstances

In the case of personal circumstances, an individual might have an underlying mental health condition, which Karate training can make worse if not conducted properly. Most people who start a martial art will have to face fear in some form. For example, fear of sparring, public performance or overcoming the fear of breaking stuff. Without positive mentoring the result of these fears might have a negative impact on a person.

Instructor

Sometimes an instructor, or the head of an

organisation, might be charismatic but lacking in understanding of the needs of students or is simply unaware of factors impacting their students' health.

If training instructions are given in a form that pressurises a student to do tasks this might lead to a negative impact on health.

Often, especially in more "traditional" branches of Karate, there can be a culture of power and bullying. This can create a mental vicious circle where bullied students either quit as they feel not worthy or tough enough to be a part of the group or result in the creation of more bullies who then take revenge on new students. This situation was recognised in the Polish army and is named "the wave". This situation is very difficult to eradicate.

This culture was very popular in Karate in the 60's, 70's and 80's. I believe that conditions have improved now, but "the wave" is not completely gone.

Group Social Setup

Karate is an activity that can make people feel that they belong to a group, which can easily turn into a sect or cult like organisation. This is a worldwide problem that sports and social clubs face every day from football, rugby, wrestling and Karate, leading people to feel that they are better than those who don't belong to the tribe.

Browsing through forums, Facebook pages or YouTube comments we can easily come across conversations or comments about the superiority of a given branch of Karate. Many claim that their style of Karate is the original one, supporting their claims with lineage, or that their system is the strongest as they <...insert whatever you want here...>.

This cult thinking can lead people into developing a delusional view of themselves as the better person. From history we know that this kind of brain washing activity can lead to the abuse of power and abuse in general. Resulting in traumatic experiences for members of that group and/or others.

Training Methods

Another factor to consider in terms of benefit outcomes is training methodology. Here again "traditional" ways can creep in, where people hold the belief that past methods are always superior to modern ones. The problem here is that even just 50 years ago we didn't know aspects of sport science, mental health and physiology in general. So, as the masters of the past relied on their knowledge at the time, now we know we can train better, safer and more efficiently.

The term traditional can also be used to hide a lack of knowledge of modern methodology, to create an illusion of exclusivity, or be used as an excuse for the barbaric treatment of students in the name of worthiness and commitment to the only true style/system.

In every aspect of life all things can be used in a

positive or negative way, Karate is no different. If you pop into a dojo and would like to start Karate, please have a look first at how the club is set up. Consider asking yourself a few questions. How is the instructor treating the students? How are the students themselves treating each other? Do the students look happy? How does the instructor refer to the competition? Search for things that are not said - the body language of people within the dojo, the approachability of the teacher, the overall atmosphere etc.

All of these aspects can give you an appreciation of the feel of the club and I would recommend that you only join it if you feel good about it and you feel welcomed. Your gut instinct is usually a great indicator of things being good or not for you.

I hope that most dojos now have moved on from being cult like and provide motivating and fun classes.

What Is Taiso?

27th of May 2016

A group of not so young people starts to gather at the hall, buzzing from the excitement, happily chatting about new moves that they are going to do today and which moves from last week they remember.

The hall is quickly filled with a group, with ages varying from 40 to over 80, dropping their shoes in the corner. Some need chairs to have a rest in between exercises but that is not stopping them!

They talk about Taiso, you know, the art of gentle exercising!

What on earth is Taiso? At LB Posture we are running classes for the not so young. I call it "Taiso – the art of gentle exercise". To create this, I have taken and modified kata from our style of Karate and added meditation music. By doing this I have a set of exercises that can be performed slowly and relaxed in the manner of Tai Chi. I do not know Tai Chi well enough to use this name but I do know Karate and have experience with kata as meditation, which is why I have researched and used the name Taiso. The word Taiso is a combination of tai (body) and so (hardening). It is a generic Japanese term for conditioning and can range from simply stretching to very serious conditioning.

I associate Taiso with exercises so my students can come along and experience training in a safe manner, learn Karate forms and enjoy them in the right state of the mind. These classes are structured with a gentle warm up, followed by learning a form and perfecting the movement. The third part of the class is dedicated to meditation, where participants perform a learnt form in a relaxed state trying to lose themselves in fluent motion. This group is not only about the exercise it is a great social platform where people can meet and share quality time. After the workout we gather and have a cup of tea and chat about random stuff.

This group was born from the need for cheap and non-impact exercises in the middle of the day so it is easier for the not so young.

Taiso has many health and mental benefits, not just working on muscles but on the brain too and helps to calm one's mental state. Via form training we can improve strength, balance, flexibility and mobility. Our brain is stimulated by learning new patterns, building new neuron connections and reinforcing them by repetition. Natural, deep breathing oxygenates blood, relaxes tension and calms the spirit. The more specific benefits of Taiso include:

- Movements that strengthen the body which helps to keep strong bones and muscle tone. Gradually students will deepen the stances increasing their flexibility and joint mobility.

- Regular exercising improves lower back strength helping to reduce any back pain.
- A frequent change of positions in different directions on one foot improves balance and hand-to-eye coordination, improving spatial awareness and helping to reduce trips and falls.
- Regular exercise improves memory and increases attention and concentration as well as brain blood flow in the region of memory.
- Taiso helps to focus on performing one movement at a time. Limiting the intake of information is a key brain function associated with brain health.
- Meditation reduces stress and improves concentration. Practice increases self-awareness. It increases happiness and meditation increases acceptance. Some studies suggest that it slows aging and the practice benefits cardiovascular and immune health.

All of the above, in conjunction with a friendly atmosphere, creates an increasingly popular alternative to what is on offer for the not so young.

- Afternote-

This group is constantly improving. At the moment we are inspiring people across Europe to follow my concept of Taiso, which makes me super happy.

Black Belt - Target or Side Effect of Training

9th of July 2016

This time I would like to write about approaches towards gradings, belt systems and the black belt. Starting with my story, I began training in martial arts when I was 14. The same as all beginners I dreamt of becoming a black belt and being able to kick ass! After 13 years I achieved my goal of attaining a black belt. By the time I achieved my black belt my attitude and opinion of what it meant had changed – I was happy to have it, but now I realised that it was not that important. During my time training in Karate my teacher did a great job of imparting the belief that it is only a belt – *"belts do not fight, they are only there to hold your Gi top together".* This was his endless mantra. Looking back, I am very grateful for him impressing this view on us.

Now I am teacher myself, I try to pass this approach on to my students and friends. Looking around I see lots of people chasing the dream of being a black belt, but they do not want to invest time and effort, they want it now, almost instantly. In this way, the black belt has become something like a driving licence. You go for a course, when you have done your hours you go for a test and if successful, receive a certificate. You can then hang this over your toilet for all your guests to admire! Then you can retire from training as you now know it all – you are the master, the black belt holder...

43

With more and more people looking for an easy way to achieve this holy grail of martial arts, there are more and more opportunistic teachers and organisations that give away black belts, for a certain price of course.

Another growing trend for extracting money from people is the creation of grading systems with up to 20 kyu grades (or more!), each of which having a separate belt colour. So, the student not only spends money on taking many grades, but also has the pleasure of buying many belts as well.

Shortening the times between examinations to 1-3 month intervals provides a steady income for examiners. Students on the other hand may experience a fake impression of progression and achievement. Such short intervals between gradings does not usually provide enough time to properly learn techniques (unless of course you are training every day for many hours). Speeding through grades at such a pace creates students who often can only remember techniques associated with the current (or very close) grade as they are constantly having to focus on the requirements for the next grade rather than building a solid body of knowledge based on an accumulation of techniques. Organisations then build black belts and instructors on this foundation. This causes a lowering of standards within an organisation and damages the image of Karate. Unfortunately, this practice has become very popular in martial arts as a means to make money. I cannot understand how students are being charged (sometimes ridiculous amounts) for gradings on top of their membership, classes and licence fees. I understand that obtaining knowledge costs time and money, but to my mind this is extortion.

In line with the realities of supply and demand, people want a black belt quickly and so other people provide this service. Having a very small dojo, I try to fight this approach. At my club we have gradings typically once a year, if (and only if) the instructor decides that a student has done enough to be graded. When permission is granted to grade, I consult my opinion with one of the other instructors within the organisation to see if they agree with my assessment of a student. If we are all in agreement that a student(s) should grade, then a grading is organised. However, we do not setup an isolated exam for only those that are being graded, but observe the students during a few hours of normal training, with a panel of instructors present. As a panel of instructors are required, our gradings often coincide with international seminars. The benefit of this is that students can be judged not only by instructors from within our own style, but also by instructors from different martial arts. All of our gradings are free of charge until black belt when there is a small fee for producing a dan grade certificate and embroidered belt.

Recently at our club we have decided not to wear belts at all as we are a small group and know each other well. We now only wear our belts when joining our friends on seminars, competitions etc. I have noticed that this approach is putting off some potential students as one of their first questions when they come through the door is *"how long do I have to train to become a black belt?"* After I finish explaining our philosophy on the subject of belts I can see the disappointment in their faces, most of them do not come back...

Another thing I have noticed recently (and is the subject of one of my previous blogs) is that people want easy training, where they pop in for classes for a bit of a workout and social interaction, but do not want to get tired. At our club our sessions are physically challenging and often involve students having to consider the details of techniques, which requires concentration and constant correction, hence my popular catch-phrase *"something like that"*.

I suspect that most people expect from their instructor a 'pat on the back' and encouraging words like *"yes, you are doing this well"*, but being from Eastern Europe I am often seen as being rude as most of the time my focus is on ensuring techniques are performed correctly. Besides, I do not like to lie and beat about the bush and so I am very direct and honest – some people do not seem to get on well with this.

In an age where everything is nearly instantly accessible, people do not often have the patience for long, hard training and being told that they are not ready to grade makes them angry. That is why McDojos are doing so well. Organisations like this have adapted to the modern, fast pace of life and fulfilling peoples demands for a quick route to black belt. However, it is my view that when we start travelling on the path called Karate our focus should be on training and improving, not on grading. In my opinion obtaining a black belt should be a "side effect" of training and not the target of training.

Confirmation Bias

20th of July 2019

Browsing through the vast number of articles, clips and conversations on forums and Facebook groups about martial arts I have noticed that a significant amount of the material covered is influenced by confirmation bias.

Confirmation bias is a fault in our thinking process. It makes us find and accept favourable information to confirm our pre-existing beliefs. Usually it is a belief that our <...insert your style or system here...> of martial art is superior to all of the others.

We have three major camps trying to discredit others - the traditional camp, the self-defence / combat camp and the sport camp. There are also cross overs and mixes between these camps all claiming that their stuff is the best. I have noticed only a handful of people who use critical thinking and accept facts as they are and do not try to stretch them to fit a pre-existing belief.

Martial artists display this behaviour when they research or remember information selectively, or when they interpret it in a biased way. The bias is stronger for desired outcomes, emotionally loaded issues and for deep beliefs.

All of the camps tend to interpret ambiguous evidence as supporting their techniques or methodology. For example, selective biased searching, interpretation and memory have been used to explain opposing views and belief perseverance even when evidence for them is shown not to be true.

Due to the fact that we all have a similar physique - two arms and legs, there are a lot of similarities between martial arts. Yet instead of finding a common ground, practitioners often prefer to close their mind and look for "evidence" to support their superiority. In response to evidence provided to the contrary they discard given information. *"I don't trust books." "I have never seen it happen therefore it does not exist."* "My master said this and that..."

I'm fortunate that at the beginning of my career in martial arts my teachers introduced us students to the concept of keeping an open mind and exploring other styles. Encouraging us to test, search and implement evidence from different martial arts. This has resulted in modifications in my Karate, where I'm constantly searching for better ways and implementing them. These modifications have come about as a result of influences from Wrestling, BJJ (sports camp) to law enforcement (combat camp) and obviously Karate (traditional camp) to improve my own efficacy.

I don't see differences between martial artists but commonality and prefer to think about us as one Tribe rather than separate camps fighting each other.

The Magic of McDojo

24th of May 2014

These are my thoughts about how standards are lowering in martial arts, especially in relation to Karate as this art is closest to my heart. Low quality dojos, money making machines and black belt factories are often called McDojos.

So, what is a McDojo? I will use this definition of McDojo by Bullshido[2] as I think the description is accurate.

"A McDojo is a school that teaches a watered-down and impractical form of martial arts in the name of making money. They place the importance of profit well ahead of teaching anything realistic or credible in terms of self-defence, and are dangerous is the aspect that they send unprepared & often over confident students into a world thinking they can fight when in actuality they have no real fighting skills.

Often McDojos teach a lot of bullshido, which is a term used to define deception, fraud, and lies in terms of martial arts. There used to be a time where a black belt meant something, back in days where it took years upon years of intense training, pain, and sacrifice. Those who wore a black belt around their waist had earned it, and they knew how to fight. Those days are gone though, and honestly, having a black belt anymore is useless.

---

[2] https://www.bullshido.net/

Who doesn't have one? With McDojos cranking out thousands of black belts to students who've trained maybe one or two years, there is no standard anymore."

In my opinion it is not always money that drives a decent club to become a McDojo, there are a few factors:

a) The number of students is overwhelming the number of instructors at the classes, which results in the lowering of standards as students do not get enough attention.

b) The head instructor has lost his/her interest and passion for martial arts, resulting in less attention and guidance for instructors and students.

c) An obsession with making black belts as a result of a keen drive to show that the club is strong, e.g. *"look how many black belts we have produced"*.

d) The creation of a money-spinning machine through frequent gradings where students are encouraged to grade when they are not ready and so have not learnt techniques properly. This results in students who have low technical standards and who cannot remember what was required for each grading, which eventually leads to black belts/instructors not knowing the basics.

All of those factors contribute to a club becoming a McDojo, so why are these kinds of places doing so well? To know the answer to this question we have to look at human behaviour. We are evolved to conserve energy like any other animal, when our brain is satisfied then it loses drive to do anymore. That is why so many of us have bought a gym membership and never gone, or maybe go once a month just so that we can say *"I have been training, I have done something"*, therefore we get rid of the feeling of guilt. The same is with martial arts with a McDojo ticking all the boxes:

a) I have done something – I went to the martial arts class so I am actually training.
b) I am not exhausted – training was not so hard that I need time to recover, I can get on with my busy life uninterrupted...
c) Training is simple – I do not have to think, I just follow commands.
d) Socialising – I have friends at the club, it is nice to meet them at training and have a chat.

So why do people end up staying at McDojos? Well, partly for the reasons listed above, but also because of not doing market research – members join a club and take for granted that they are being taught by experts. This is an odd behaviour as most people would never do this in other situations. For example, when buying a car, we do not tend to just go to one car dealer, look at one car and just buy it, we tend to look at multiple cars, test drive them, weigh up the benefits etc. So why in martial arts do so many people just come through the doors of the dojo and never check other clubs? I am still looking for an answer to this one...

At my club I always recommend new students go and explore other clubs/arts around. Sometimes new people never come back to my classes and I am happy that they must have found something that suits them. So many teachers say to their students that they should not go to other classes as *"we are the best",* however in many cases this may be paraphrased as *"don't go looking elsewhere as they might be cooler than us!".*

I have been training with my two teachers for over 17 years now because they have always been open minded and encourage me to explore all roads in martial arts.

I hope these few words will make people recognise and consider the consequences of training at McDojos.

Outsiders

16th of August 2014

Throughout my martial arts journey, I have been lucky enough to meet some extraordinary people, excellent teachers and great friends. Most of them have one thing in common - they are what I call "outsiders". I will skip mentioning their names as I am sure most of the people who know me will know who I am writing about.

An outsider is a person in martial arts who does not belong to a big organisation, usually by choice. The reason for this is simple; the outsider does not want to have to deal with the politics inherent in a large organisation. In some cases the outsider is driven away from an organisation as he stands up for what he thinks, which sometimes results in a conflict with the leader(s) of an organisation. This non-compliant behaviour can lead to them being side lined.

I have had the honour to meet many outsiders over the years and I can say that these are the people who have influenced my martial arts the most.

Although outsiders are by definition on the fringes of martial arts that does not stop people in a large organisation from exploiting their knowledge, but in my experience it is often the case that the outsider does not get any credit. For example, a few years ago a group in Poland were accepted into one of the biggest Karate organisations in the world. This group were advertising themselves as experts in kata bunkai (applications). However, what was not mentioned was that their top instructors had asked an outsider to teach them about kata and their applications as they were worried about being able to pass their grading in front of a highly ranked Japanese teacher. After these instructors passed their gradings their ties with the outsider were immediately cut without so much as a thank you or recognition that he had prepared them for their gradings. This example of where an outsider is essentially used when convenient is not an isolated case and I believe this is because outsiders tend to be devoted to their art and are therefore happy to help wherever they can, without looking for fortune or fame. I also believe that this situation is not unique to martial arts, but occurs in other sports as well.

For years I have been observing these behaviours and have tried to avoid them with reasonable success. I have sometimes found myself being dragged into political games, but fortunately for me it did not take too long to notice the situation and act. Having left these games I have become an outsider myself and I have to say that I am very happy to be in this position as it gives me the flexibility to cooperate with whoever I want, regardless of their affiliations. I no longer have to comply with nonsensical rules or pay for membership and other fees to make the businessmen happy. Although it would not be fair to say that being an outsider means that I am completely free from problems. As larger organisations tend to turn into money making machines they become very introverted and do not want to cooperate with anyone else. Hopefully this will change in time. To try and encourage better interaction between organisations our small group of outsiders get together regularly at seminars and deliberately make them open to all that are interested. At these events we can meet and train with other teachers and hopefully meet likeminded people.

In a bizarre way most outsiders are naturally attracted to other outsiders, in this way I have made friends around the globe and across the sports and arts, gaining opportunities to train with great people. Those outsider teachers that I know and cooperate with often do not have to force people to respect them as by their actions they earn respect. I have seen this pattern repeating in multiple systems such as Karate, Ju jitsu, Kung Fu, Kempo, Aikido and Wrestling.

I have decided to write these few words as for nearly 20 years in martial arts I have seen these situations occurring over and over again causing stress to students and teachers, but not many people seem to express their opinions on this topic. So, there you go, here is my small opinion. I should add that my opinion about organisations is based on my personal experience and does not apply to all of the associations and groups out there.

This might be controversial to some people who I know but all of us know what we carry inside, maybe some people who will read this will find their inner outsider.

Funakoshi's Anxiety?

23rd of February 2018

This article is just my speculation...

The other day I was going through one of Master Funakoshi's books, The Essence of Karate[3]. In reading it one sentence really caught my eye.

"As a child, I suffered from a very weak stomach until I started training in Karate..."

When I think about it, I too had a very weak stomach until I started Karate. I know that there is no medical data that identifies for certain what condition Master Funakoshi may have had, but I know what was wrong with me.

A weak stomach can be a symptom of anxiety, self-doubt and lack of confidence, as it was in my case. Consequently, my theory is that Master Funakoshi also suffered with anxiety prior to him beginning his training at the age of 13 and that Karate helped him improve his mental health, leading to physical wellbeing.

"Once I started Karate, however, it would seem that my ailment was afraid of Karate, as it disappeared, and I have not succumbed to illness for even a single day since that time."

Working with students who suffer with anxiety like myself I can see how Karate training and positive

---

[3] Funakoshi, G (Reprint Edition 2013), The Essence of Karate, Kodansha America, Inc.

reinforcement from instructors can improve a person's mental wellbeing. It does this by boosting self-confidence and helping to emphasise self-worth through a structured progression. Given my experience perhaps Master Funakoshi's revelation that Karate cured his stomach weakness prompted him to promote Shotokan Karate as a holistic system of self-development and self-improvement as well as a martial art.

If my speculation is correct then I believe that this would be the first documented case of Karate helping to fight a mental health condition through structured training methods. For me this seems quite plausible and would be seen as a positive demonstration of Karate practice leading to health benefits.

- Afternote-

Some time after this article was published, I decided to abandon the massage therapy part of my business as it had become too stressful for me. When I was unable to help a client I could not switch off and was constantly trying to think of a solution. This was negatively impacting my mental health and family life, so I decided to drop this work and focus on Karate. This is when I made the decision to transform 'LB Posture Training' into 'Les Bubka Karate Jutsu'.

"It's easy for you, you're a personal trainer"

"It's easy for you to be fit and healthy, you're a personal trainer!" Erm, not so much. I often hear this statement used by my clients who believe that being fit comes easier to fitness professionals. However, let me just explain my reality and how I became a personal trainer and therapist in the first place.

In a nutshell, it all happened as a result of me trying to resolve my own injuries and imperfections, but let's start from the beginning – my right ankle.

When I was a young boy I was (apparently) a promising goalkeeper at one of my local football clubs and had the potential for a career as a footballer. Unfortunately, this dream was cut short as a result of a cycling accident. I had been riding around my neighbourhood and fell from my bike, spraining my ankle. It was pretty painful, but after a quick visit to A&E it had seemed to be on the mend, or so I thought. After two weeks in a cast the pain was unbearable. I was in tears and it felt as though the cast had been shrinking, squashing my ankle. My dad decided to take the cast off to release the pressure and then take me to the hospital. To our horror, my ankle was now yellow and had swelled to be three times the size of my other one. We went off in a panic to the hospital where the doctors took me straight into theatre to operate as it transpired that my ankle had started to rot and had turned into a huge abscess. As a result I had to spend two months over the summer holidays in hospital following the removal of over a glass of rotten fluid and some fragments of my ankle bones. Along with parts of my ankle, my hopes of becoming a footballer had been taken away from me.

To this day the consequences of this accident still give me problems. My right ankle is weaker and less mobile than my left and the lack of stability of the ankle joint forces my calf muscle to compensate, causing me stiffness in my lower leg as well as knee pain.

Moving onto my shoulders... When I was 15 I developed an interest in weight training. All of my friends had started building muscles and so I too dreamt of becoming a body builder. Being a teenager, it is natural to be rebellious and alas I was no different. So, when the gym instructor said to start training with smaller weights we were all of the opinion that this was just a waste of time, after all, we wanted to be big and strong now! So instead we went for the maximum weights that we could lift. This approach worked very well – until a few years later. Over these initial few years my strength grew significantly and whilst I only weighed 55kg I could bench press 105kg. In hindsight I now realise that I really should have stuck with small weights as to this day if I try and perform a bench press with a significant weight my shoulders just say *"no!"* and I get a pain that feels like someone is trying to rip my arms off. I still enjoy weight training today, but I now train with moderate weights and have switched to functional training with kettlebells, which reduces the pains and aches in my shoulders.

Then there is my beloved left knee. During my time training at the gym I discovered my biggest passion, Karate, which I still actively engage in both training and teaching. As young students we did not have much understanding of body mechanics and how to train smart, all we wanted to do was to train hard and non-stop. This resulted in me pulling one of my tendons (ACL) in my left knee. After consultation with a doctor he suggested I have an operation to fix it. Given my previous ankle operation experience I was less than keen with this approach and so decided to seek opinions from a variety of other doctors. I came across a sports doctor who advised me to keep walking for as long as I can on the knee as it is and to avoid the operation. That was 14 years ago. I still have problems with my knee, but I have created my own strength programme and mobility workout that helps me get along and enjoy a largely pain free walking existence. Although occasionally I take a wrong step and my knee just collapses, taking the rest of my body with it. These situations make me focus more on the postural aspects of my training.

Lower back pain, yet another issue. At a similar time to when I damaged my knee I started to experience lower back pain. Going back to the doctors again I was faced with a now familiar story – we need to operate as we have diagnosed that you have narrow nerve channels in your lower back. I was like *"what?"* There was no way I was going to risk my ability to walk to get rid of this pain. I would rather be in pain than bed bound. After many visits to different doctors it turned out that there was a simple solution to my problem, which maddens me even now to think that so many doctors were so keen to operate! One of the doctors I saw simply looked at my gait and told me to invest in a good pair of shoes that will stabilise my ankle and hold me upright. Et voilà! After buying a decent pair of shoes my lower back pain eased off.

Finally, there are my upper back problems. Being an experienced martial artist, I decided to broaden my skillset and joined a Wrestling club, which I still visit whenever I can. Wrestling is full of acrobatics, which is awesome when it goes right... However, with me being confident that I was invincible and could perform any stunt I decided to prematurely try to perform a back flip without assistance. I had been warned that I might get hurt as I was too inexperienced, but I knew better so I tried anyway. I failed big time! I landed on my head and it felt like my spine had been crunched and was falling apart. When I got up I had troubles with breathing, lifting my arms up and moving my head. It felt like I had been interrogated by a medieval inquisition. Surely someone had just put a metal band around my chest with two spikes pointing at me and had started to tighten it! Another visit to the doctors, but following an x-ray that did not show up anything I was told to rest for a few days, take some pain killers and all will be fine. Well, all was not fine and I spent seven years in pain whilst doctors told me to get used to it as there was nothing wrong with me. Nothing wrong? I could barely move my arms above the height of my shoulders, how could this be normal? I had lost hope that I would ever have this issue fixed, but by chance I met a martial artist, who is now a close friend, who used his Chinese massage therapy on me and within a week the pain was gone. I was so grateful and so intrigued by his methods that I decided to become a Therapist and to help others like me who are being told to just get used to the pain.

All of these injuries and experiences have led me down the path of becoming a Personal Trainer and Therapist, not in the search for riches, but in a search for self-help. Through my experience I feel driven to help others and can empathise with what my clients are going through. It is not always easy to find a fix. My battle with my own body has been ongoing for more than 30 years now and along the way I have tried a range of conventional and unconventional methods and am able to appreciate what has and has not worked for me.

It is easy to assume that people who are currently fit are able to achieve/maintain this state easily, but you never know what their story is. It is very difficult for me to keep motivated to do workouts and mobility drills and present a cheerful character at all times, but whenever I slack and slow down my body starts to fall apart. That is quite a good motivator for me to continue to study and complete my workouts.

Best wishes from a self-fixing Personal Trainer and Therapist.

Why I don't like Boxercise

29th of July 2016

Please note that this article is not intended to criticise individual instructors, but rather a comment against the current system of education and qualifications in pad work. I love training and teaching pad work routines. Using pads is an integral part of martial arts training and brings great benefits. It is a great way to improve fitness, coordination, strength and self-confidence. My issue with Boxercise and other similar systems is the time it takes to become a qualified instructor. Being able to hold pads and being able to punch pads are two sets of skills and to become skilful in anything takes time. To be able to effectively teach these skills requires experience as well as knowledge of teaching in either 1-2-1 or group situations.

In browsing through social media I have noticed a surge of instructors offering pad work. From the images and videos I have seen it appears as though they have very little experience of how to hold pads safely. Seeing the way that they hold these pads raises the question in my mind why are they teaching? It turns out that to qualify as a pad work instructor typically only requires a one day course – that is why they are teaching. However, being able to obtain an instructing qualification quickly extends beyond the realm of pad work. When I did my PT qualification we received 4 hours of kettlebell training. After this we were assessed on what we had learnt and having passed this assessment all of the participants on my course were qualified in kettlebell instruction. I found this slightly surprising and so I spoke with my classmates about their confidence in teaching kettlebells. Most of them said that they did not wish to teach kettlebells because they had no prior experience and did not feel that the training they had received was enough for them to feel confident in teaching others correctly.

In my opinion this system of having just a 4-8 hour course to train instructors will sooner or later result in injury. Recent studies suggest that the shortest time it takes to learn a new skill is 20 hours[4], with more traditional views suggesting it takes 10,000 hours to master a skill. Certainly, in the case of martial arts I think 10,000 hours is more realistic – I am not aware of anyone who has been able to proficiently learn a martial art in 20 hours! Even the fast learning systems implemented in organisations such as the Army to fast track soldiers to be combat ready take 140 hours.

As an example of the types of areas covered by these 1 day instructors courses please find below an extract from the Boxercise website of the topics covered in 1 day:

---

[4] For example: https://first20hours.com

- *"Punches – learn and practise the eight fundamental punches ensuring correct & safe technique. Learn the importance of good footwork and stance.*
- *Group Work Section including instructing skills & Boxercise Aerobics*
- *Boxing Equipment Discussion and good practise recommendations. Class format and design.*
- *Pad work – Learn all the relevant safety and coaching points for using the focus pads. Also learn how to coach every punching fault so you are prepared for when it occurs in a real-world situation.*
- *Assessment – Working in pairs you will be assessed on your ability to coach, teach and instruct a novice puncher and demonstrate all punches safely and effectively. Pass mark 70%.*
- *Class Examples of four different styles of Boxercise class, including bootcamp style.*
- *The Boxercise Instructor Course includes footwork drills 1-17 for the Boxercise Footwork Training System."*

This is a lot to learn in one day, especially when you consider that you then have to be able to teach someone else. I have been practicing martial arts for nearly 20 years and have been on both sides, as the puncher and as the pad holder. Based on my experience I would definitely say that to be proficient at either takes more than a day.

Instructors often post pictures from their training sessions and from these you can notice basic mistakes such as holding the pads too high or too wide. From this you can deduce that the holder does not have sufficient tension in their arms to prevent injury. It is also not very realistic for the person who punches – unless they are fighting with a very tall person with two heads. Another common mistake I have noticed is the pad holder doing all of the work, smashing the gloves of their client. This may sound and feel stronger for the client, but it does nothing for his/her fitness.

Here are some points to avoid when holding pads:

Too high

Holding the pads very high causes a lot of stress on the shoulders as muscles are not able to provide support to the arm when receiving a punch in this position. This is also bad for the person punching as they do not learn realistic targeting. The pad holder should keep the pads at an appropriate height for the target such as the head or body in relation to their build.

Too wide

Holding the pads in an unrealistic position where the pads are too wide apart can cause the person who is punching to overstretch and slows down their technique.

In the same way that holding the pads too high causes stress on the shoulders, holding them too wide does as well. The pads should be held within your own shoulder width at the appropriate target position (head or body).

Relaxed

Keeping your arms relaxed is dangerous for both the pad holder and puncher. The puncher does not get any feedback about their technique and risks hyper extension whilst executing a punch due to lack of resistance. Conversely, without tension in their arms the pad holder does not have much control over their muscles in order to protect their joints when receiving a punch, which might easily lead to injury.

Hitting oncoming punches

Many instructors hit the punch of their client with the pad in order to make it sound and feel more powerful. By doing this we create a false distance for the target and cause unnecessary impact on the joints of both the holder and puncher. This behaviour teaches the puncher to shorten their technique and therefore they cannot develop full power. There should be a very slight movement towards the punch just before contact so that your joints can prepare for receiving the impact, but this movement should be minimal.

Lack of instruction

It is not enough to just ask the client to punch with a particular combination. You have to actively monitor and correct his/her technique throughout the workout. For example giving tips on footwork, striking technique and body mechanics. The instructor should be looking to spot errors at all times, but in order to do this he/she needs experience in punching and body mechanics.

In summary good pad holding helps to:

- Prevent injury to the pad holder and puncher
- Establish the correct distance for each technique
- Enforce the use of proper body mechanics
- Improve punching skill
- Support a smooth transition between punches

All of this takes time and practice. As with other manual skills, our brain and muscles need time to develop neuromuscular patterns. In my opinion a few hours on a course does not provide enough time to attain these skills and in this article I have only touched on the basics. There is a lot more to consider in pad work such as punching technique, structure, moving, progression and use of different types of pads. It is such a vast topic that it is not surprising that great pad holders are paid top money for their instruction. They spend years developing their approaches.

Chapter 4 - Philosophy

The philosophies expressed in this chapter are inspired by the work and teachings of many people that I have had a chance to cross paths with. For example, Tadashi Nakamura from Seido Karate, Dietmar Schmidt from Zendo Ryu Karate Do, Artur Marchewka from Shin Ai Do Karate and many more. As I have matured as a teacher, I have evolved my own approach and elements of this have developed into my philosophies toward martial arts and life in general.

Ko Gaku Shin - Keep Your Mind Open to Learning

10th of December 2016

Keep your mind open to learning. We must remember to constantly learn and study, always be a student...

As we continue to expand our knowledge and become an expert in our field, no matter if it is our work, hobby or Karate, we can observe an interesting aspect of a master, or an expert in his chosen field - they are characterised by a hunger for knowledge. Not only in his/her speciality but in all directions, everything is interesting and can improve their understanding of their subject.

In Karate we can translate that approach into looking and learning from other martial arts and sports. We can potentially find something anywhere that will help improve our technique, and if we do then we should utilise it. However, having an open mind does not mean that we should always look outside for learning. There is no replacement for repetition, practice and self-discovery, you might be shown a technique by a lot of teachers, you think you understood it and practiced it a hundred times. One day you unexpectedly performed this technique perfectly and then the realisation comes that all those times before you had been wrong.

This process will continue to happen after hundreds of repetitions then after thousands and then after a million. Learning through repetition helps gain understanding and confidence. The technique becomes a part of you and you will tailor it to your body and mind. You will understand that no one gave you the answer, you have found it within you. This self-search, experimenting and confidence in having an open mind is a key to mastering Karate and other disciplines of life

Kenjo No Bitoku - Virtue of Humility

Unpublished Article

In Karate our goal is to make our bodies as powerful as possible and our spirits and characters strong. Yet a strong body without humility can be used inappropriately, over confident, ignorant of others. Lack of humility might lead to bullying, and disrespectful behaviours. Training in Karate with humility makes us realise that we might have strong bodies, but we are relatively weak and fragile, we are powerless against time, diseases and other accidents. Humility helps us to build a strong moral spine and to be confident but not overconfident, always striving to help others and care for others. A Karate student should always keep in mind that he is strong but weak, this approach provides a healthy perspective of oneself in relation to the surrounding world.

Omoiyari – Caring About Others

31st of December 2016

"Strong and caring people are the pillars of society and Karate helps cultivate them."

Omoiyari is one of the Japanese expressions that is very difficult to explain to a non-Japanese person. Some say it is thoughtfulness or as Sugiyama Lebra defines Omoiyari *"the ability and willingness to feel what others are feeling, to vicariously experience the pleasure or pain that they are undergoing and to help them satisfy their wishes... without being told verbally"*[5]. For me personally it means simply caring for others and myself.

This type of caring is sincere and not motivated by reward, we care for others without seeking compliments or gratitude. If we help others expecting an acknowledgment with a 'thank you' we are not having Omoiyari and we do this for the pure purpose of building our ego.

That is why I encourage my students to be helpful to anyone in the dojo as we are like a family where we all support each other, but this care is not limited to the dojo; we need to care about and help people everywhere.

---

[5] For more information about the Omoiyari concept I recommend this essay: Tshering Cigay Dorji (2009), Omoiyari - A Japanese Lesson, Kyoto International Cultural Association Essay Contest (http://kicainc.jp/english/contest/essay2009-2.html)

I often see, especially in big dojos, students training in isolation not willing to interact or share their knowledge and experience with anyone. We all need to train hard but some Karate practitioners come to a dojo with the attitude of *"I'm here to train, to better myself and I'm focusing on myself"*.

This is not the right attitude. This type of training creates strongly egocentric people who in life are so busy focusing on themselves that they ignore all others who might be in need. What we need in society are more empathetic people who can help others. Through Karate training with Omoiyari in mind we can achieve this.

Fu Gen Jikko – Action Speaks for You

19th of December 2016

In every aspect of life we meet people who say *"Don't worry you can count on me. I'll be there."* However, when it comes to take action they do not due to a change in their circumstances.

The same situation occurs in the dojo as many students make big statements such as *"Sensei, I'm going to be the best student ever. I will train hard and will not miss any classes, just watch me."* Then invariably something gets in the way. Work, family or health issues arise and so the student is unable to keep his promise. I used to believe in all of these promises and it would raise my hopes. Nowadays I am bit more reserved and just wait. I know that people mean well, but I cannot understand why there is this urge to announce that we will take action?

One's actions are the truest expression of one's character. In our dojo we encourage people to act rather than just verbally promise. Making a statement is easy, but it can hurt the feelings of others and discourage trust as the promises are broken. Unfortunately in modern society this seems to have become a norm. For example, a lot of customer service organisations will promise to call you back and sort things out, but never do. We have all been there! Karate encourages students to be reliable and trustworthy via the practice of Fu Gen Jikko.

The Enemy Within

6th of March 2016

Turning up at the dojo, just before training starts I can sense the enemy around. He is waiting to strike. The class lines up and starts the initial ceremony, shutting our eyes in meditation, he is here creeping around us.

Training starts and as we go through the kihon the battle commences with my worst enemy. The enemy within. The voice in my head that whispers *"you have done enough, you don't need to do those punches, no one will notice"*. We move on to partner training – *"take it easy, you know this stuff, you don't need to try"*.

Then on to sparring – *"give up, you don't need to fight, you did well in the first bout"* and so on... All students will face the same enemy, which is why Karate is a way, "do", for self-development. If you can win with yourself you become strong. We need strong, self-confident people.

Being confident means that you are not afraid to stand up for yourself or for others, which enables us to take action and to help. Strong and honourable people are needed in a healthy society and Karate is a tool for creating individuals with a strong spirit through hard training.

Modesty, Kindness, Honour and Diligence

4th of May 2015

Modesty, kindness, honour and diligence – all of these qualities should go with being a black belt or master of a martial art, but are these behaviours actually being reflected? The more I am exposed to martial artists, the more I doubt it.

When I started doing martial arts nearly twenty years ago, I was naive in believing the myths that masters possessed perfect characters and were akin to knights from fairy tales. In my young mind a black belt (master) should be a super being that floats along the ground on a cloud of perfection, without a mark on his reputation.

Within a few years of training in martial arts my dream of the black belt super being was shattered and left in tatters. I am not talking here about the technical aspect of being a master of a martial art. This is a completely different matter that I could write a whole book on.

In this article I would like to focus on a master from a moral point of view. Maybe I should start with myself. As I wear a black belt some people look up to me to be the 'knight in shining armour', sorry to disappoint but I am only human and I certainly have my faults! There is nothing wrong in not being perfect, but my issue is with people who pretend to be perfect and preach to others on how to behave.

I have been lucky enough to have had the opportunity to take part in a large number of seminars with a range of instructors from 1st Dan up to 10th Dan. I often leave these seminars with mixed feelings. Some people are genuine and modest and do not try to be someone other than who they are. Others try so hard to show themselves in the best light that it is sometimes painful to watch...

I cannot understand how some demand instant respect for being a master (yes, we should obviously respect everyone as a person) as this kind of respect is earned through actions not demands. From my observations it appears that the more insecure a person is the more respect they expect. Individuals who know their value do not need to pretend that they are perfect and are more open to criticism.

On kindness, with my curiosity in all martial arts I do tend to ask a lot of questions and I have been taught by my teachers to not hesitate in asking questions of higher grades in a direct manner. Through this approach I have had the opportunity to see how top martial artists behave and this gives me a chance to form an opinion on their kindness (their willingness to share knowledge and their tolerance of me asking questions). Based on my observations given the people that I have come across I would suggest that there are not many kind people in martial arts (I am more than happy to be proved wrong if all of the kind martial artists out there would like to make themselves known!). A lot of them seem to have the belief that *"I'm better than you; I've got a higher grade"*. Some of the reactions that I have come across when engaging with higher grades includes:

- An expression that suggests *"how dare you speak to me"*, as he is a master.
- An expression or verbal question that implies *"who is this person and why are you asking me questions?"*
- Blunt responses to my questions – presumably in the hope that it will get rid of me.

It is a rarity to find a master who is very friendly, chatty and open (but when I have previously found such people we often become good friends).

Unfortunately, it seems that the more seminars I attend the more instructors I see that demand to be praised and are less and less approachable.

With regards to honour, having been engaged within the martial arts community I have seen all kinds of fights/struggles over politics, power and money (or 'martial arts hell' as I call it). It seems to be getting worse and even those who I thought I knew well and respected have suddenly changed their tune – chasing the power and not taking any prisoners. Not to mention the common behaviour I see of people trying to discredit other instructors who have different opinions and ways.

As a result of my experiences I cannot help but think that we really should not use terms such as 'honour' and 'kindness' etc. in relation to black belts or masters. Whilst these qualities may have been appropriate in the past they appear to be dying out in modern society, perhaps as a consequence of being able to sail through grades at the speed of light... Those who are modest will probably agree with me that the titles and grades are not worth the hassle and that they do not need to prove their value to anyone.

I wish that you (as well as myself) have the opportunity to meet genuine teachers with open minds.

Loyalty

3rd of June 2016

On a previous training session I discussed the topic of loyalty in martial arts with my students.

The definition of loyal[6] is: *"Faithful to any leader, party, or cause, or to any person or thing conceived as deserving fidelity."*

From this we can see that you can be loyal to a leader, cause or a person/thing. So, which one would be applicable in the case of Karate? Your teacher, style or maybe just to Karate itself? How to choose so as not to upset anyone?

In my experience the most common form of loyalty in martial arts is to the first two – loyalty to a teacher or to a style. Some people get very angry when their student tries someone else as their teacher or trains with another system(s). I believe this stems from a fear and insecurity of the instructor or organisation, or just selfishness, but I will not dwell on this as it has not been something that I have experienced with my teachers.

Instead I would like to focus on how I see loyalty in my club and with my students. This is nothing new and it has been embedded in me by my teachers, for which I am very grateful.

I expect from my students that they be loyal to themselves, to follow their gut feelings in martial arts.

---

[6] Definition taken from www.dictionary.com

Their best guide is their own intuition, which will give them ideas and concepts to follow so that they can achieve their maximum potential. However, with this type of loyalty I also expect them to be honest with me. Not because I want to know what they are planning, but because maybe I can help and guide them to the best possible teacher, saving them the effort of following dead ends that I or my teachers have followed before.

From my perspective the more important aspect of loyalty is that of the teacher to the student. As a teacher I have to provide my students with assistance for them to find their path through martial arts. It is my job to indicate to them other options not just Shin Ai Do and to encourage them to ask questions and to try other arts and teachers. Being loyal to a student is to not judge them on their actions and to understand that they are going through a process of self-development and self-discovery. To be honest I have been going through the same process myself in martial arts for nearly 20 years and I have certainly made some mistakes along the way.

I expect my students to not be afraid to come to me and tell me that they are going to other clubs, teachers and/or organisations. Honest behaviour makes me proud of them and saves us all any unpleasant feelings later. I will not stop any of my students from following their own way and I hope that we will always remain friends.

In my view respect has to be earned from both sides. You earn each other's respect by following your passion and by being honest. From my perspective as an instructor I am more than happy to see that a student has found their ideal art/activity elsewhere and will encourage them to try it out, with the knowledge that the doors of my dojo will always be open to those that showed the respect and courage to do what is best for them.

Being loyal does not mean to be blindly following a teacher or organisation, it is to follow your own passion with respect to your teachers and mentors.

"Karate should be Fun"

24th of December 2015

Browsing through Facebook I have come across this quote, *"Karate should be FUN"*, by Jesse Enkamp. I don't agree with this statement, I believe that Karate should not be *"fun"*. Let's start by looking at the definition of fun. Fun can be said to be:

- Enjoyment, amusement, or light-hearted pleasure.
- Playfulness or good humour.
- Behaviour or an activity that is intended purely for amusement and should not be interpreted as having any serious or malicious purpose.

In my opinion Karate should be hard work with a focussed mind, with the practitioners focus being on one thing – training. Karate can be rewarding and enjoyable but after training. During the session you are committed to pay attention, to be focussed and work hard.

When we have fun, our mind is not focussed, it wonders in enjoyment and pleasure, and therefore it cannot execute techniques with concentration. Performance decreases, awareness drops and people become relaxed and careless, which can lead to injuries or bad technique.

I have never heard a committed athlete who has achieved success say how fun their training sessions are. Instead they say that all of their hard work has paid off.

When people look at martial arts as a way to just have fun their achievement levels are not likely to be high as they lack focus and the drive to work hard. There is nothing wrong with a bit of fun but please don't call it a martial art.

- Afternote-

In the past few years I have eased off somewhat on my vision of strictness in Karate. In a relaxed environment we learn faster, but that does not mean we should be too relaxed. Training should be a fine balance between humour, focus and hard work.

The Moral Spine of Karate

9th of June 2016

When I started my training in martial arts I did not think about all of the culture, rules and traditions – *I just wanted to kick some ass!* As I was always one of the smallest on my estate I tried everything to make myself bigger and to be able to fight. So I started going to the gym and I joined a Karate club. I had a clear vision of being just like Bruce Lee.

Moving forwards 20 years and I now appreciate all of the rules, traditions and morality associated with The Art of Empty Hands, especially the aspect of "Do". Looking around I find that the emphasis on the moral aspect of martial arts appears to be decreasing. Quite a few teachers seem to promote aggression and the disrespectful behaviours of macho men/women. Good examples of this can be observed in the worlds of Boxing and MMA where fighters try to dominate their opponent before they even step into the ring, making as much hype as possible around their persona in order to generate more money. Two fighters who highlight this particularly in my opinion are Connor McGregor and Ronda Rousey. Both are exceptional fighters with excellent skills, but they are extremely rude to and about others. Behaviours like this puts me off from watching MMA and makes me question whether these famous fighters are the best role models for young people? I personally do not think they are and I have more respect for an average fighter who has respect for others. He might not be at the top of his profession but he is a humble hero who promotes the best behaviour for the young people that take up martial arts classes.

From running my own classes I have noticed that people are drawn to moral martial arts where you can learn honour, diligence and respect and how this fits in with traditional systems such as Karate, Aikido, Ju Jitsu and others.

For me the philosophy of Karate works, giving people that train not only a physical workout, but in addition teaching them a structured, moral code. This is the essence of the phrase *"Karate ni sente ashi"*, *"Karate does not attack first"*. The name Karate "Empty Hands" is telling in itself in that it signifies that empty hands are about protection and that the hands being open is a welcoming gesture. Karate should be used only for good reasons with respect to others and in case of danger to self or others.

Kaicho Nakamura has pointed out a few key principles in Karate that really resonate with me and that I try to impose in my training and life so that my existence is meaningful and helpful:

- **GI** - **Rectitude** – To take the right decision in every situation and to do it without wavering. The right decision is the moral one, the just one, the honourable one.

- **YU – Heroism** – Bravery means taking risks to our position, status or self-interest on a daily basis.
- **JIN – Compassion** – We should always try to find ways to express our compassion for others.
- **REI – Courtesy** – We should practice it constantly especially in modern times where we are lacking in courtesy.
- **MAKATO – Truthfulness** – In all dealings with others, we should develop a sincere, honest straightforwardness.
- **CHUGO – Devotion** – always be devoted to your family, friends and teachers.

The above are great tips for an honourable life. I guess the question is how many of us follow them in our lives once we step out of the dojo? We can hear in the media about martial arts instructors scrounging on benefits, molesting children and taking people's money. It is easy to preach about honour, diligence and respect on classes and then get involved in corrupt behaviours and doing harm to others. Many instructors want to be perceived as holy, without a mark against their character. We would all like to be like that, but reality is often different. We all have faults, but we can strive for perfection through our choices and actions. I do preach about honour and respect and I have to confess that I am not always perfect, but I try to follow the path of Karate do, self-education and excellence. Since I started to employ these principles I have noticed that my life has changed for the better and I am now helping others through Karate. I wish for all instructors to be an excellent example to their students, we certainly need more respectful people in this world.

Be Yourself

A lot of people that I teach try really hard to be someone else. In their eyes they should be like pop or film stars or like fitness models. I too have been guilty of this, striving towards and pretending to be a better version of myself. Unfortunately, this way of thinking leads to nothing good as we will always have this internal battle between our true self and the false projection. You will never know what potential you may have until you release your true you. Since I stopped worrying about who I wanted to be and started to be the person that I truly am my life has blossomed. I do what I love, I'm with who I love and I'm enjoying life. Most importantly my life has started to come together and I'm successful, perhaps not in the eyes of others, but in my own, which makes me an incredibly lucky man. I like this quote by Oscar Wilde a lot:

"Be yourself; everyone else is already taken."

Here is a fable about a 'cracked pot' which describes how we are short-sighted and not seeing our true potential and purpose.

"A water bearer in India had two large pots, each hung on each end of a pole which he carried across his

neck. One of the pots had a crack in it, and while the other pot was perfect and always delivered a full portion of water at the end of the long walk from the stream to the master's house, the cracked pot arrived only half full.

For a full two years this went on daily, with the bearer delivering only one and a half pots full of water in his master's house. Of course, the perfect pot was proud of its accomplishments, perfect to the end for which it was made. But the poor cracked pot was ashamed of its own imperfection, and miserable that it was able to accomplish only half of what it had been made to do.

After two years of what it perceived to be a bitter failure, it spoke to the water bearer one day by the stream. "I am ashamed of myself, and I want to apologize to you. "Why?" asked the bearer. "What are you ashamed of?" "I have been able, for these past two years, to deliver only half my load because this crack in my side causes water to leak out all the way back to your master's house. Because of my flaws, you have to do all of this work, and you don't get full value from your efforts," the pot said.

The water bearer felt sorry for the old cracked pot, and in his compassion he said, "As we return to the master's house, I want you to notice the beautiful flowers along the path." Indeed, as they went up the hill, the old cracked pot took notice of the sun warming the beautiful wild flowers on the side of the path, and this cheered it somewhat. But at the end of the trail, it still felt bad because it had leaked out half its load, and so again it *apologized to the bearer for its failure.*

The bearer said to the pot, "Did you notice that there were flowers only on your side of your path, but not on the other pot's side? That's because I have always known about your flaw, and I took advantage of it. I planted flower seeds on your side of the path, and every day while we walk back from the stream, you've watered them. For two years I have been able to pick these beautiful flowers to decorate my master's table. Without you being just the way you are, he would not have this beauty to grace his house."

Be yourself no matter what flaws you may think you have, others might take them as your most valued qualities.

Life Purpose – What would you do if...

11th of May 2016

A few days ago I was visiting one of my friends. I love to talk to Marek as he always has something interesting to say. This man always has his own opinion on any subject and I don't know many people as knowledgeable as this bloke – he is run by an urge to know everything!

When we meet we like to talk for hours about philosophy, different views on life and current events. I respect Marek for other reasons too. He is painfully honest. He will say what he thinks no matter how upsetting this might be for you. Maybe because I am the same that is why we love to talk to each other.

This time Marek asked me a question. It was a very intriguing question. He mentioned that when speaking to other friends not many people can definitely answer it. He was sure I could as he described me with *"You are different"* I didn't know if I should be happy or worried. The question was this:

"If there was no limit to money what would you do in life?"

Damn this is a good question and he was right. Without thinking I answered that Karate is what I want to do, to be precise, to help people through Karate.

Marek exploded with *"I knew it! You are one of the*

most focussed people I know and you are realising your goal". Again he is right as I do teach Karate to help people of all ages.

This conversation made me think about it and as time goes by I can see that there are so many people traveling through life without clear purpose, they do not know what they want to do.

Another thing that I have discovered since I had developed my clear vision of who I want to be and I have started realising bit by bit my dreams is that I have I stopped expecting outcomes. I enjoy doing things just for the experience of doing it. I have to say that my life has become less stressful and more enjoyable now, and I can really say that I'm happy.

I hope that more people will find their purpose in life and can achieve their dream. Sometimes what we need to see things clearly is another person's question with their point of view. I love to chat to Marek, he's such a nice guy.

Overthinking and Mindfulness

23rd of May 2015

This Thursday, after a couple of weeks break from training, we were back in the dojo. I have to say that I had recently lost interest in martial arts and was struggling to find the motivation to create a training programme – it felt like my interest was falling apart. By coincidence we were not able to train for a bit due to a trip to Poland to visit the family, illness of members and our training hall being used as a polling station. I think it was fate giving me a rest from training tiredness. Recently I found myself overthinking the state of the club such as the drop in members training, which led to thoughts of closing down the club and focussing on my work.

It's funny how life leads us on to greater things. As a part of my work I had the opportunity to attend a meeting with therapists like myself from all different backgrounds from meditation techniques to manual therapies. I spent about three hours listening to the different concepts and how each can help us. I came out of this meeting with a completely clear head, free from worrying about the club's future. As one of the ladies said *"Overthinking the future is stressing and when life is stressing you who do you think will win, you or life? I'd put my money on life, so stop worrying about the future."* What great advice.

Another thing that changed my approach was examining quotes that were selected at random at the meeting, prepared by a Mindfulness therapist. The quote that I got was *"The most important point is to be really yourself and not to try to become anything that you are not."* (Jon Kabat-Zinn). I don't know why, but these two pieces of advice sit perfectly together in my mind, so after consulting with club members it was decided that we will carry on with training sessions. However, there will be a few changes to make it more affordable such as reducing the class time to one hour per session. With fewer people training we can increase the pace of each session, focus more on technique and stick to a more structured programme.

I have now found a new wave of motivation for martial arts and have developed programmes for the various classes. In the last session there were only four of us, but everything went very smoothly and was logically interlinked with kihon and bunkai complementing a physical workout. I have not enjoyed a session as much for some time. By not overthinking and sticking to who I am and how I teach I am able to make the sessions so much more enjoyable for me and therefore for my friends that train with me. In this way we are happy to be a small, quality group who just enjoy training. Whatever the future will bring we will be there standing tall and ready for it!

"Black belt is the beginning" - is it?

9th of July 2016

Obtaining a black belt is just the beginning of studying Karate. How many times have you heard this phrase? When you get to be a black belt, then you will learn the important stuff... In some ways I do agree with this statement, but in others I don't. How can the achievement of a black belt be the beginning when we have spent years training and mastering the basic techniques in order to get it? By saying that 1st Dan is just the beginning, shouldn't we just start as a black belt? Or should we forget everything that we have learnt when we become a black belt? In terms of a schooling analogy should we say that attending University is the beginning of learning and forget about everything we had learnt at primary school, secondary school and so on?

I describe the 1st Dan black belt as an intermediate level, one where you have a solid foundation and can now progress your Karate in your individual way. In this sense you could say that it is the beginning of your unique direction in Karate, based on what you know you can interpret it and mould it in the way that you want.

Sometimes I listen to instructors and I get the impression that they use the expression that *"a black belt is just the beginning"* as justification for not teaching their students properly and trying to keep them in the dojo. I know quite a few black belts who were disappointed with the lack of progression achieved by being promoted to 1st Dan. The result was that they quit their training, their argument being that they were not learning anything new. So how can this be the beginning? There are a growing number of instructors who have been told that after attaining a black belt they will learn more, but they never did. However, as we often mimic our own teachers, these instructors continue to promulgate this view.

In the case of my teachers, when you reached the stage of 1st Dan you are enrolled in a research programme to find your own way in Karate, experimenting with different ways of performing techniques and digging in to anatomy, physiology and psychology. A black belt in our organisation must have their own identity and should not be just a copy of his/her teachers.

In summary, I believe that a 1st Dan black belt is not a beginning, but a progression from basic to intermediate understanding, which is just a step along the long road to perfection...

I Hit Sensei

9th of August 2019

A few recent events and conversations at the dojo inspired me to write this article.

The first event was during a sparring session when one of my students delivered a lovely, spot on, spinning back fist that nearly took my head off. The second was during another sparring session where I had a good rear naked choke on a student. As he was doing a good job of getting out from it I allowed him to escape.

I didn't think that either of these situations were unusual until we started to chat about it afterwards. I have to mention here that many of my students are already experienced martial artists and so have backgrounds of training and gaining achievements in other clubs.

What was surprising for me was their reaction to these events. In the first instance, after this lovely back fist my student got scared. I was puzzled, why would she be afraid? So I asked *"what's wrong?"* She replied *"I'm worried that now you'll punish me like my old sensei did."* I replied *"why would I punish you? I'm congratulating you as you delivered a perfect shot at the right time, it was superb."* She asked me if I was not embarrassed that a student had hit me in front of the rest of the class? Well we'll get to that a bit later.

The second situation was similar. The student had a

previous background in martial arts and he was puzzled, asking why didn't I finish him? I had the opportunity to do so. His previous teacher had always done that, showing him that he was a lesser fighter than the teacher.

I don't attempt to criticise other instructors as everyone has their own methodology of teaching. My view on this is that as a coach I try to point out the best in my students, and the way to do this is to support, motivate, and praise them but to also be honest. If they do something incorrectly, I let them know. If something is done properly, they are always acknowledged. This applies to all training aspects from kihon to sparring. As a coach I have to leave my ego outside of the dojo for the benefit of my students.

My approach is to get the best out of students. When I see that they have an opportunity to execute a correct technique no matter if it's a strike, kick, lock or choke, I allow them. It doesn't make me weak or embarrassed and gives motivation to my students that they can get me. Don't get me wrong, I'm not easing off but I make it possible with effort to achieve. Always making sure that I praise them for their achievement. I don't get upset if a student, regardless of their grade, will catch me with a great punch and I don't need to get revenge or punish them. I enjoy their progression as it shows me that I have taught them correctly.

As someone who suffers with anxiety, this is one of the few areas that I feel confident that I know my value and I don't feel embarrassed or a lesser man if a girl with a white belt will choke me out, she simply did a good technique.

This approach builds trust between a coach and a student. Students know that no matter what they will be treated with respect, building the right behaviour model when they spar with someone else in my dojo. No one is trying to show superiority and all of the students and instructors respect each other. This attitude makes me proud to be a part of a great team of likeminded people.

Do not "Osu" me please!

14th of June 2014

Across Karate dojos all over the world we can hear the term "Osu" being used for all manners of expression, from greetings to acknowledgement or even goodbye. Some people use this expression outside of the dojo, for example in shopping centres, cinemas, BBQs etc. when they see someone from their dojo. However, how many of us have really put any effort in to understand the meaning of Osu?

For years I was using it in my dojo without really paying any attention to it, as our style is an offshoot from Kyokushin Karate and so everything is Osu! The only difference for us was that we did not use it outside the dojo. My teachers have always said that we are not in Japan therefore there is no need to use it. For me personally it feels awkward when I meet someone in Tesco and I am "Osu-ed" at, my answer is always *"hello, how are you?"* Some people just ignore this change others ask me why I do not reply Osu!

These kinds of situations make me think that maybe I should find out more about Osu. I started to talk about it with Sensei from different martial arts, and most of them informed me that it is a rude and impolite expression and is used by "common folk". Some people explained to me that it is used in the army and that is why Mas Oyama incorporated Osu so much into his

Kyokushinkai.

Whichever origin is true for Osu, the common opinion is that it is not polite and should only be used in friendly groups, but not everywhere.

Kano Paradox – Art vs Sport?

9th of August 2014

Which approach in martial arts prepares us better for self-defence – traditional or sport?

This question often causes a lot of debate with traditional martial artists explaining that life threatening techniques are more useful in real life situations due to their dangerous nature. Examples of these techniques might be eye gouging, striking the throat or attacking the groin. On the other hand, we have combat sport, where the opinion is that sport is better to defend yourself as constantly repeating drills gives rise to an automated response to a dangerous situation. To have a clear view on this matter I would like to have a look at the definitions of three aspects:

- Traditional martial art
- Combat sport
- Self-defence

I will define each of these terms in turn.

Traditional Martial Arts

Traditional Martial Arts (TMA for short), is the branch of martial arts that focusses on artistic expression along with preservation of the old ways, customs, and philosophies. As with all fighting arts traditional forms often have valid combative applications, but are frequently taught with an emphasis on self-development and / or self-perfection. At the moment there is a growing movement of practical TMAs, like Karate, returning to their roots of self-protection.

Combat Sport

In Combat Sports the main focus is on the competitive side of training with the cultural aspects of the art often being dropped. Most of the training is grounded by the rules of the sport and so revolve around competition constructs and scoring systems. These rules can promote one feature of the art over another, for example placing emphasis on wrestling, boxing, kicking, aesthetics etc.

Self-Defence

Self-defence is a term that is sometimes misused or misunderstood. In this context it is used to describe various systems that prescribe ways of dealing with a combative situation where there is a physical attack. Within this group we have systems that deal with situations such as civilian combat, law enforcement, and military. Each of these systems have different objectives, but none of them are concerned with aesthetics or traditions. They all focus on the best possible resolution for the problem being faced.

Within TMA we have lots of 'mysterious' moves, deadly techniques which executed properly will give us the advantage over an attacker. However, as there are so many of these moves there is not enough time to train in them all to make them become a spontaneous response to an attack. Another problem is that it is not possible to repeatedly train these techniques – I cannot imagine anyone would be willing to join a club where the students regularly test their deadly strikes on one another as we might have more students seriously injured or hospitalised than at training.

Combat sports are different in that there are no fancy movements. Everything is efficient and has the sole purpose of winning the competition and all of the training structure is dictated by the rules of the game. Constant repetition of combinations and drills results in the development of muscle memory and subconscious responses. This gives an advantage over an attacker, but the rules of the sport also get imprinted in our brain and this may be a disadvantage. For example, training in a knockdown fighting system a student may not be in the habit of punching to the head (because this is not allowed in competition) and subsequently is not used to being punched to the head either. The existence of these rules can result in a student being used to a referee intervening when a foul has been committed. All of this can work against us in a real-life confrontation.

Self-defence teaches very direct techniques to damage an opponent without strict rules. Subconscious responses are a priority and survival is the main goal. However, from my experience most of these self-defence groups pay less attention to fitness development. Some groups that I have met also promote a psychological setup where their students believe that after two weeks of training, they will be able to win in a confrontation or will be able to disarm an attacker with a knife or a gun. This is unreal and might even put the life of the student at risk.

So which one is better? There is no definitive answer to this question as it all depends on the individual.

Getting back to the title of this article of Mr Kano and his paradox and leaving self-defence systems aside let's have a look at how this paradox was created.

The question of *"which is better traditional martial art or combat sport?"* was asked to Jigoro Kano (the creator of Judo) as he removed all dangerous techniques from his Judo and focussed on sports methods. In 1886 in Tokyo a Police tournament was organised of *"real fighting"* where students of Kano were challenged by masters from traditional schools. Some of the masters were from Yoshin Ryu, a leading school of Jujutsu. Of the 16 fights Judo players won 13, proving that Judo is better in a real fight. This is the Kano Paradox in that Jigoro Kano had managed to create a combat sport that worked better than the traditional 'deadly arts' by removing all of the life and health threatening techniques.

As I am doing both an art and a sport, I have views from both sides and like to mix all the benefits and concepts from sports and traditional martial arts. Prior to starting wrestling my only martial art was Karate and so I had focussed more on the traditional approach to self-defence. Unfortunately, during this period (in my late teens) I was unlucky enough to be involved in a few incidents on the streets of Krakow. Some I lost and ended up with bruises and a broken nose, but most I won and so I believe that Karate did give me an advantage over my attackers. Now that I am older and living in a quiet neighbourhood, I have no need to focus only on self-defence and so can enjoy the art of Karate and free sparring in sport.

I would recommend that people just train in whatever programme gives them the most satisfaction, and not to worry about self-defence as I would hope that in reality very few of us are ever attacked. Any form of sport will give benefits in case of a confrontation as being proficient in sports builds confidence. This confidence sends a signal to a potential attacker that *"I am fit, strong and not a victim"*. In any case, if we are attacked it is likely that our primal instincts will take over, which will use maybe 10% of our skills... The rest is all down to our gross and fine motor skills under stress. In this way it all comes down to the individual – some people who have never trained in martial arts/combat sports are excellent fighters when under stress and end up winning on the street whereas we see some great masters and boxing champions being beaten up.

- Afternote-

After training more with combative systems, I can now see a trend of mixing traditional values into combative systems, in order to keep students engaged in training. An example of this would be Krav Maga, where the original training programme was designed to be completed in 140 hours. A lot of Krav Maga schools now have a belt or grade system, and their syllabus has been expanded so that it almost resembles that of Karate. I would also argue that a lot of TMAs today take part in their own competitions and there is currently a renaissance of self-protection in Karate, where there is an ever-growing interest in the combative application of forms.

Chapter 5 - Techniques

This section is dedicated to the technical side of Karate with specific examples of technical performance. I examine some of the anatomical and physiological details of movements and explain why I teach or do certain things the way that I do. I also explore some of the concepts within Karate that are evolving and changing.

Muscle Memory

23rd of August 2014

Instructors in martial arts very often use the term 'muscle memory', but they often cannot actually explain what it means. In this article I will try to explain my views on this topic.

I will begin with some definitions for muscle memory, motor skills and subconscious reactions.

These definitions have been taken from Wikipedia.

"Muscle memory has been used synonymously with motor learning, which is a form of procedural memory that involves consolidating a specific motor task into memory through repetition. When a movement is

repeated over time, a long-term muscle memory is created for that task, eventually allowing it to be performed without conscious effort."

We have two types of motor learning relating to Gross motor skills and Fine motor skills:

"Gross motor skills involve movement of the arms, legs, feet, or entire body. This includes actions such as running, crawling, walking, swimming, and other activities that involve larger muscles"

"Fine motor skills are the small movements that occur in the hands, wrists, fingers, feet, toes, lips and tongue. They are the smaller actions that occur such as picking up objects between the thumb and finger, using a pencil to write carefully, holding a fork and using it to eat, and other small muscle tasks that occur on a daily basis."

Subconscious reactions:

"Occurring without conscious perception, or with only slight perception, on the part of the individual: said of mental processes and reaction."

As we can see from these definitions our muscles can learn or maybe it is better to say that they can synchronise with the brain to perform tasks, with maximum efficiency. This learning process increases the speed at which we can execute practiced movements, which is why when we first start to learn how to punch or kick our movements are sluggish and clumsy. With time and repetition our moves start to become quicker, stronger and more precise. These moves become more natural and we do not need to concentrate so hard on how to perform them.

All of this is due to our system of connections between the brain and muscles via a network of nerves. Our nervous system is a bit like a muscle, when put through training it gets stronger and bigger; our impulses can travel quicker as the amount of connections dedicated to each of the tasks is increased. In time our brain also learns how to recruit more muscle fibres to support a movement.

Our brain creates a plan of action which can be performed by our muscles, so we are able to perform defending or attacking combinations. When we develop muscle memory our ability to perform these tasks improved.

In the context of martial arts however there is a slight problem with muscle memory. Whilst it allows us to perform a task quickly and is good for predictable situations in martial arts every situation will be subtly different. The dynamic nature of fighting makes it difficult to know what will happen next and be able to plan a prescribed response.

That is why it is so important to develop subconscious reactions, where we do not have to choose the right move to block an attack. Our brain should be trained to switch between tasks without thinking about them. It is a kind of muscle memory for the brain to spot small signals and to choose the appropriate reaction for our muscles. A good example of this will be how we automatically protect our eyes. When an object is travelling at speed towards our eye, we do not think to close our eyelid; it happens much quicker, our hands travel up to catch the object or cover our head without thinking about it. We are usually able to think about what happened after the event has occurred. This kind of response is what we are looking for in martial arts. If we can master our response to stimuli without the involvement of conscious thought we will become better fighters. This state of mind is called 'Mushin', which means an empty mind in Japanese.

Combining an empty mind with muscle memory allows us to easily switch between defence and attack, deciding which technique to use in a split second.

In summary, muscle memory is a combination of brain activity synchronised with muscles via a network of nerves.

- Afternote-

In this article I have got it wrong. In hindsight I most probably rushed through it and did not check the facts. We cannot compare the automatic reaction of an involuntary system to a trained voluntary system. A much better comparison would be fighting and driving. I think for most experienced drivers, we drive by habit, and are not fully paying attention to what our body does during the drive. Karate should become the same hardwired actions, taking you to your required destination.

A Simple Way to Improve Kata Understanding

1st of October 2016

For a traditional martial artist the word 'Kata' has a defined meaning, but for those outside of martial arts it can be a confusing term. Kata is a Japanese word that means 'form'. In Karate this form is a set of movements that are performed in a sequence. All of the movements replicate self-defence techniques without the need for an attacker to be present.

Kata represents a codified platform of possible self-defence applications. The process of analysing these applications is known as Bunkai.

In most Karate schools students learn Kata in order to progress through a grading system. The most common teaching mechanism is to learn the Kata pattern first, master it, and then move onto the analysis of the movements by breaking the form up into its constituent applications. This is a very quick way of teaching the pattern and works on the principle of *"monkey see, monkey do"*.

This method of teaching results in students learning very crisp moves with the consequence that their flawless techniques look more like a dance than a martial art. It is beautiful to watch, but often you can see that they really do not appreciate or understand the Kata. The reason for this is that when you have engraved a pattern in your brain and muscle memory without a practical application it is very difficult to then adapt those moves to a self-defence situation that would work on a resisting opponent.

This is because our brain is unable to easily make the leap from the perfectly performed technique to one that takes account of variation in the moves of an attacker. I have found that for those students that have been taught Kata without the applications struggle to make the switch to performing a Kata that is effective in reality.

In my dojo (another Japanese word that literally means 'place of the way' and is commonly used for a place of training) I adopt a different approach to teaching Kata. I start by teaching the application so that students are shown how and why the techniques work, then we move onto the pattern. In this way it is easier for students to visualise what they are doing at any given point in the Kata. In this way I try to involve students in the practice of an application on a partner so that they can understand why Kata is important, which is aligned to the following Chinese proverb: *"Tell me and I'll forget; show me and I may remember; involve me and I'll understand."*

A drawback to this method of teaching is that the performed Kata is not always so sharp, as the techniques do not need to be perfectly executed in order to be effective.

Once students understand the Kata we can then work on polishing their techniques. In order to do this we have three ways of performing a Kata, which are interchangeable.

- **Technically correct** – to the best of the students ability.
- **Slow** – with maximum tension and strength.
- **Fast** – without concentration on the technique but focusing on the pattern.

Combining these three approaches stimulates the body in different ways, which helps to improve all round technique, speed and strength.

As this is my preferred way of teaching, my Kata is often described as ugly or technically inferior to other systems, but I don't mind as I know that my Kata works.

Is doing basics always good for you?

5th of July 2014

"Doing basics is always good"

I have heard this so many times! It is often used by instructors all over the world as an excuse, to cover their lack of advanced knowledge. From a Karate perspective I would consider basics to be the standard Kihon – single techniques that are executed in a repetitive fashion. I can understand those who wish to perfect a single technique through years of dedication to the art of movement.

For most practitioners, how long does it take to learn the basics? Are you ready when you graded as a black belt to do advanced stuff? Probably you will hear *"now you have to master the basics"*. It is a bit of a phenomenon in martial arts, as you have never been told in school *"OK you have learnt the alphabet, now go and master it!"* You initially learn the alphabet so that you can progress on to reading and writing words, which then leads to sentences and so on. I have never heard of someone who is already literate going back to learn their ABCs… As a comparison, in martial arts you learn the basics, then you do combinations and kata, but then you are told go back to basics. I guess I have been very fortunate to have teachers that have encouraged me to do more advanced training and have always supported me in looking for someone who can teach me more.

Regressing back to basics is a common practice in martial arts. Having visited seminars with high grade masters with 6th, 7th, 8th dans it has always seemed odd to me that we do basic techniques such as tsuki, mae geri etc. for hours. I personally disagree with this approach, yes from time to time we need to refresh our memory by going through basics but basics from a certain grade upwards cannot replace quality advance training. In my club, students from about fifth Kyu are introduced to more advanced concepts of Bunkai (applications) and Kumite (fighting). Having become dan grades, our students should attend regular advanced classes that do not repeat basics – basics can be done at home or when teaching other students.

I believe that after attaining black belt we should switch our focus from technique in favour of adopting a way of thinking. What do I mean by this? We have all been told that this technique is for this or that. For example let's take Soto Uke, which is taught as a block for an incoming strike. Yes you can use it like this, but there are multiple techniques that you can use for blocking a strike. Perhaps more useful applications of Soto Uke is as a take down, high throw, joint lock etc.

What we aim to achieve with students by getting them to adopt a way of thinking is to stop them worrying about specific techniques for specific attacks and shift the emphasis to responding fluently and automatically to a threat.

When we start discovering all the advanced applications for basics the reason why we are taught them in the first place becomes clear, with the result being that we change the way we execute the basic technique to suit its application to each threat that we are faced with. Every student will begin to tailor their basics differently as we are all built differently and think in different ways – we often have our own favourite ways of doing things.

So to conclude, we need to have a solid foundation in our basics in order to progress, but if we do not make this natural jump from basic technique repetition to understanding their advanced application then we are missing out on a big part of the depth of our art.

I hope that you found this article helpful. I think the practice of basics is a contentious issue as lots of people have their own thoughts on how to effectively incorporate them into training. I look forward to further debates on the issue!

Breath in Karate

2nd of December 2016

Breathing is one of the basic functions of our body, our autonomous system. We do not have to learn how to do it, we are born with this ability. If you look at a baby breathing you can see there is no struggle, breaths are easy and full, its belly moves rhythmically with every breath.

When we grow we seems to forget how to breathe fully and healthy, our breath is changing becoming shallow and quick. Air in our lungs is not fully exhaled, preventing us from having a full inhale of fresh air. In this way we are only using a third of the actual volume of our lungs, decreasing exchange of oxygen and carbon dioxide, therefore our brains and other organs are never fully oxygenated. Most of us breathe with the upper parts of the body. This type of breathing is called intercostal breathing.

In Karate just like in meditation we try to focus on diaphragm breathing. In Karate the centre of the breath is in the Hara or Tanden, a spot about four fingers directly below the navel. Breathing with hara requires good posture, our spine is elongated, our abs relaxed, the diaphragm is stretched and pulled down, and when we inhale our belly pushes outwards.

Exhaling compresses the stomach, pushing the diaphragm upwards and forcing the air out of our lungs.

When we are relaxed we should see rhythmic waves of our stomach in and out.

In Karate we have two types of breathing:

Meditation (relaxed)

Inhale – breathe in through the nose. Centre your breath in the stomach letting the breath in naturally without using the abdominal or chest muscles at all.

Exhale – breathe out through your mouth. The lips should be slightly open and your tongue elevated. Let your stomach fall back in and breathe out slowly, double the length of the inhalation. When you feel that all the air has left your lungs squeeze gently the lower part of your abdomen.

This type of breathing is very helpful for relaxation and calming down, it is use in meditation and medicine. The principle of a longer breath out than breath in is used in the prevention of hyperventilation, for example in women giving birth.

Ibuki (power generating breath)

Inhale - through the nose rapidly, filling up your lungs from bottom to top, using your stomach.

Exhale - tense your abdomen muscles, open your mouth wide, with your throat open and your tongue relaxed and held in the lower palate. Squeeze from your hara (point blow the navel) and keep breathing out loudly till your lungs are completely empty then dynamically squeeze the rest of the air with a small cough.

This type of breathing is used to develop power. You often hear Karate practitioners make a loud noise; this is a Kiai. This is the same type of breathing but faster and in time with a technique to generate the most power. This technique is used also by weight lifters to generate power.

Zen masters say that to relearn the natural way of breathing takes around six years and it is an art in itself.

As in learning all skills experience is the key to understanding and it is gained through individual practice under an experienced teacher and the right atmosphere in a dojo.

Components of a Punch

In this article I would like to focus on the components of a front punch. I will try to describe the basic mechanics of our body when punching. Our interest will focus on the following four key points of our body:

- **Fist** - positioning the fist in relation to our target and the natural set up of the wrist and knuckles.
- **Elbow** - the setup of a safe position to make use of our body's natural cushioning mechanism and effective transfer of energy.
- **Shoulder** - in relation to our target and our hips, allowing the most power delivery.
- **Hips** - angle of the hips when striking to improve power transfer.

I will skip leg setup and the use of the back and front legs. I will come back to this in another article.

First we have to look at the natural set up of our arms, trunk and hips. As you will probably have noticed our limbs when relaxed are not fully extended, this anatomical adaptation is to protect our joints from injury. We try to replicate this setup when punching. To understand this natural setup let your arm drop to the side of your body in a relaxed position and have a look in a mirror to see this natural posture. Now clench your fist. You should be able to see that your shoulder, elbow and wrist create a 'zigzag' pattern. Now if you raise your arm and point to your target you have a safe and proper setup arm from shoulder to wrist.

Why is this setup the best? All of the bends in our joints (especially the elbow) create a cushion. When our fist impacts a target a shockwave is generated that goes through the target and back through our arm. A bent elbow allows us to absorb this energy - if we had our arm completely straight, all of the energy from the shockwave goes directly up our arm to our shoulder, which increases the possibility of damaging our joints.

Fist clenching - there are a few schools of thought on this and I will focus on the two methods that are best for me.

- The first method is with all of the fingers tucked in with the thumb covering index and middle finger.
- The second method is with the index finger resting on the base of the thumb. As a result of this change the thumb is now only covering index finger. This setup gives me a firmer base for the front knuckles, but it is a bit slower to do.

The rest of the setup for the wrist is the same for both fist methods. Looking from the top of the fist we should notice that fist is not straight but bent outwards. Why? If we had our fist straight the punch would be delivered by only the middle knuckle, which might cause unwanted movement in the wrist and sprain it. There is

127

also no cushioning effect. When the fist is bent both the first and second knuckles land on target, giving the most efficient transfer of energy with maximum stability.

Another very important angle is the vertical wrist position in that the wrist should be slightly bent downwards, which results in the fist dropping slightly. This position allows us to land two knuckles when punching at head level or higher. By bending the wrist we expose the knuckles. If we have our wrist vertically straight our punch will land with the middle joints of our fingers, which may cause injury. Note that there is a technique where we hit with these knuckles (hiraken), but the position of the hand is changed significantly to provide support for this.

Now onto the elbow. The elbow's relaxed position is at a slight angle – if we relax our arm, the elbow rarely straightens completely. This is our body protecting our joints. When we punch we want to use this mechanism for our benefit. Apart from the safety risks, having a straight elbow when punching causes our shoulder to turn towards the centre of the body as the shoulder is unnaturally lifted up, which results in power loss. This elevation of the joint also tenses the trapezius and neck muscles which reduces the speed of the punch. To insure the most powerful strike our hips must be directed towards the target. This allows the direct transfer of energy through the trunk, shoulder, elbow and wrist to the target. If the whole system is correct we will have minimal losses in energy transfer.

If we turn our hips too much we will increase the reach of the punch, but it will lose a lot of energy as the hips provide the direction for the power. A simple exercise to test this is to place your fist against the wall in a punch position. Now push your body weight into the punch with your hips directed forward. You should feel supported by the two first knuckles of your fist with your shoulder in a comfortable position. Shifting your hips towards the centre of the body (pushing the fist further forwards) causes the rotation of your trunk and you should feel the change in direction of the energy. Moving your hips changes the direction in which the shoulder is pointing as it moves with your trunk and so the energy is directed in line with the hips. Therefore the punch does not impart the maximum power. This position may also cause shoulder injury.

Ideally, the hips should be directed to the target (for a front punch) and lifted up to help with the contraction of stomach muscles. Then the energy of the punch will flow through the shoulder, elbow and wrist, exploding via the first two knuckles.

I hope this explanation will help with understanding the components of a punch from a Shin Ai Do Karate point of view.

All of the mechanisms described here are best tested and trained on a makiwara (punching flexible board) or a heavy punch bag under the supervision of qualified instructor.

How to - *Mae geri – Front Kick*

26th of July 2014

One of the most common kicks in Karate is a front kick or 'mae geri' in Japanese. In this article I would like to provide my take on how we perform mae geris in our style.

There are a few ways of performing this kick. The two most common are:

- Mae geri keage, which is quick, powerful and snappy.
- Mae geri kekomi, which is a thrust kick.

Both of these methods are useful for different situations. From these two basic methods we have a few variations like a stopping kick, a toe kick, a kick that changes trajectory as executed and so on.

In describing these kicks, let's start with the body mechanics. Mae geri is a kick to the front and our focus is to deliver most efficiently maximum power, to do so we need good posture, appropriate muscle contraction and accuracy.

There are a few variants of foot positioning within this technique. Nowadays the most popular form is kicking with the ball of the foot, where the toes are pulled back upwards.

In the old days the preference was different, with some schools preferring to use a foot position where the toes were pulled back in a similar fashion to the fingers of a fist.

In my opinion this was a very dangerous way of performing this kick as the toes are very fragile in this position. Older Okinawan styles use the tsumasaki method, which hits with the top of the toes.

Personally, this is my favourite way of kicking. The small surface area created by the top of the toes makes for very painful kicks. This method needs practicing and conditioning to be able to perform it properly and safely. This setup works great when wearing shoes in a street confrontation.

Another often used surface is the whole sole of the foot (mostly in kick boxing). This setup gives great support for stopping kicks or stamping.

Given that mae geri keage is the most popular form of front kick in Karate I will focus on the mechanics of this method.

Starting with a proper base for the kick is very important, some Karate styles teach that the supporting foot should face straight forward when kicking. From my point of view this is less powerful and reduces freedom of movement as our hips are closed and therefore block each other. From anatomy we know that our hips open up when we walk, that is why our feet turn outwards to allow the maximum range of movement.

We want to take advantage of this range of movement when kicking. By doing this we have quicker, stronger kicks with a longer reach and the additional benefit of not putting stress on our supporting knee.

When kicking without a target (in the air) we must concentrate to make sure that we do not straighten our knee as this dynamic movement is bad for our joints.

When we execute a mae geri we do the following:

1. Turn our supporting foot outwards (opening our hips).
2. Raise our kicking knee up whilst bringing the heel of our kicking foot towards our glutes (stretching our quads, which provides for a more explosive release of the foot as we kick as the quads go back to their natural tension). Aside from making our technique powerful and quick, by raising our heel up to our glutes and our knee to our stomach we essentially hide our foot from our opponent and then as we kick in a straight line it is difficult for our opponent to see. This is because our eyes have evolved to detect motion from side-to-side at a distance (to identify potential threats or prey), but we are not good at judging the distance of an object moving directly towards us. As we raise the knee we also pull the kicking hip back slightly, as we execute the kick the hip will rotate forwards bringing more speed to the kick.
3. We make sure that the supporting leg is little bit bent, as this gives us stability.
4. As we move the foot forwards to strike the target, we ensure that our foot position is set (depending

on the type of kick we decided to use) and that the foot muscles are tense to protect our joints. As mentioned in point 2, as we kick our hips move forwards to help drive the kick forwards.

5. As we hit the target we tense our leg, back and stomach muscles to help transfer energy into the kick.

6. Keeping the knee up we then pull back the kicking foot. This pull back should be even quicker than when we drove the foot forwards. This is partly to create a shorter impulse of energy, which is more painful, but also to ensure that our leg is not caught by our opponent.

7. We then place the foot back down.

Some common mistakes that occur when people kick a mae geri is that their upper body is leaning too far forward or back. Leaning forwards too much makes us vulnerable to a punch in the head. On the other hand tilting back too much will make it impossible to tense our stomach muscles and keep balance. If in a fighting position, it is also important for us to keep our hands protecting our head.

Mae geri is a great weapon in fighting and can be used in different ways, as an attack, for defence or as a distraction. We can perform it on the move forward or backing up and it can be snappy or thrusting.

I hope you found my description of a mae geri useful, however describing how to kick is no replacement for feeling how a kick works for you through training and under the supervision of a good instructor.

In teaching Karate I see a lot of students struggle with kicking, moving and standing in stances. Whenever I discuss this with people they say that it is due to a lack of flexibility. Most of them focus their efforts on improving their flexibility. So they stretch and stretch, but without the desired progress. This is often because they have forgotten about mobility. Only through both increased flexibility and mobility can we improve our range of motion, but we cannot do one without the other.

The next article will focus on exercises for improving mobility in the ankles and hips with detailed descriptions of the movements that I use as a part of my corrective exercises.

Flexibility and Mobility

21st of May 2016

Our ability to move within our range of motion is determined by the physical structures of our body. These structures are the tissues that surround our joints, which allow specific movements. The muscles have to stretch and relax to some degree to allow movement. This has to be accompanied with the ability to use and activate appropriate muscles at the right time and in the right order to adopt a correct position. Different muscles have different jobs to do within the motion of a joint. Some will drive the movement, others will assist or stabilise and whilst others will stop the movement once the joint has reached its end of range of motion.

We can see that flexibility is a highly dynamic action that will require a series of coordinated and sequenced muscular responses. It is about being sufficiently mobile, that is *"having freedom of movement"*[7], which needs stability to control the movement of that joint. Increasing the static flexibility of muscles will not see an improvement in these qualities/abilities.

"Joint Integrity must never be compromised for range of motion. The goal of flexibility training is to functionally lengthen and strengthen."[8] (Vern Gambetta)

---

[7] Collins Dictionary

[8] Vern Gambetta (2002), extracted from Postural Analysis and Corrective Exercise (PACE) Manual (2013), Premiere Training International.

For a joint to have a high level of mobility it must have a high level of stability to control the movement within its limits. If the joint has weakness within its range of motion then the body will limit that range of motion with other structures in order to protect itself.

"The ability to functionally take advantage of just the right amount of motion at just the right joint in just the right plane in just the right direction at just right time."[9]

The optimum ability of a joint occurs with the right amount of movement and an appropriate amount of stability provided by the joint and muscle tissue.

To improve the range of motion within a joint it is necessary to conduct repetitive and appropriate exercises using the right methodology. It is extremely important to work on strength to control the newly developed range of motion within that joint.

"Repeated movements can be used therapeutically to produce desired increases in joint flexibility, muscle length, and muscle strength, as well as to train specific movement patterns."[10]

Mobility is the key to performing efficient movements in Karate. Freedom of movement allows you to execute the correct technique with the least amount of effort. In my teaching I use sets of exercises

---

[9] Gary Gray (1996), extracted from PACE Manual (2013), Premiere Training International.
[10] Shirley Sahrmann (2002), extracted from PACE Manual (2013), Premiere Training International.

developed by therapists and personal trainers to increase mobility and reduce the probability of injury. Please find in the following a small selection of exercises. Note that detailed workouts are designed on an individual basis following a postural assessment of movement patterns.

Mobility Exercises

Tightness in a joint is caused by our body trying to protect it. Only once our body feels stable and strong throughout a joint movement will the new range of motion be possible as the body's protective mechanism switches off and neural over-activation of the surrounding tissues subsides.

Muscle tissue has to be able to control a wide range and type of movements and conditions. Therefore, exercises should mimic these factors:

- Light
- Heavy
- Slow
- Fast
- Simple
- Complex
- Isolation
- Compound

In martial arts we increase the range of motion by working on:

- **Static or partially loaded movement** – isometric, stable and controlled exercises through full range of movement
- **Bodyweight** – gravity load from slow to fast movements
- **Complexity** – combining movements from other parts of the body or changes in planes of motion
- **Progression** – adding resistance, repetition and reducing rest

Ankle and Foot Mobilisation

1) Leg Swings

Stand leaning with your hands against a wall. The back leg is straight (no bend in the knee) and the ankle is nearly at the end of its range of motion, with the heel firmly on the floor. In this position raise the front leg off the ground and swing the leg from side to side in the same fashion as a pendulum (yoko keage). The front leg should be nearly straight with the foot passing through the centre line of the body as far as possible on either side. Continue to swing the leg in a controlled manner, enabling the supporting foot to pronate and supinate, without lifting the heel.

Figure 13 - Leg Swing Exercise

2) Driver

Kneeling on one knee, place the elbow on your front knee and shift your bodyweight forward so as to flex the front ankle. Use the elbow to drive the front knee forward and the calf muscles to return. Try to cover all of the directions of the front ankle's range of motion (to the left, right, forward and so on), all without lifting the front heel.

Figure 14 - Driver Exercise

Hip Mobilisation

1) Shifts

Stand with one foot on a raised surface with that leg straight. Lift your hands up over your head and gently drive the arms towards the straight leg whilst at the same time driving the hips towards the supporting leg, which is slightly bent at the knee. Return the hands to centre and repeat again with control.

Figure 15 - Shifts Exercise

2) Squat

Stand with one foot on a raised surface. Squat down whilst reaching your arms forward at hip level. Make sure to keep the back straight. Return up and repeat.

Figure 16 - Squat Exercise

Pelvic function

1) Kneeling Overhead

Kneel on one knee; this will be the side that will be worked. Lift your arms up and gently drive the hip (on the working side) forward and then back. When driving the hip back lower your arms in front of your body to shoulder height. Repeat the forward and backward motion with the arms moving up and down.

Figure 17 - Kneeling Overhead Exercise

2) Step to Overdrive

Place one foot on a raised surface with the instep of the foot on the surface. Lower the supporting leg into a squat position whilst raising your arms overhead. Return to the starting position and repeat.

Figure 18 - Step to Overdrive Exercise

Joint mobility is starting to become more recognised as an integral part of improving body movement and posture. As a result, more and more martial artists are becoming aware of its importance. I will be teaching aspects of improving mobility at the Isshindo Kan International seminar that I will be attending in Mrozy, Poland next month.

Use of Gedan Barai - Lower Parry

30th of April 2016

In this short article I will look at a way in which we use Gedan Barai in our school. There are plenty of applications for this technique. Some use it as a block/parry or, as in our case, as an attack. There is no right or wrong way to use Gedan Barai, just whichever works best for you.

Let's go through the movements of this technique and their uses. At the start of the sequence we place one arm in front of us with a fist whilst the other arm travels up to the opposite ear. This second arm then sweeps downwards, clearing anything in the way.

This way of executing the technique is the way it is performed in kihon and is just a movement at this point. The technique is transformed when you imagine the function of every part of the movement and then test this vision on a partner that is first willing to cooperate with us and is then resisting.

For this demonstration we will be working on a defence from a double grab. For this application the first move is transformed into a punch to the abdomen. Depending on which arm is used this punch will be either to the spleen or liver. The second arm that travels upwards will then be used as a strike to the head (with the hand opened or closed). This strike is targeted at the ear, temple or vital points on the jaw . Note that when a technique causes us to touch a part of our own body this often indicates where we should attack our opponent.

When our strike connects with the head of our attacker our elbow proceeds to come close to our body, trapping the arms of our opponent. The arm then continues to travel down to unbalance our attacker and open him up to our counter attack.

In reality the first and second arm movements are done simultaneously.

I hope that this description demonstrates our way of thinking about kihon and how it is used.

Thigh Kick - Mawashi Geri Gedan

4th of October 2014

This article covers how to perform thigh kicks or in Japanese, Mawashi Geri Gedan. Around the world different martial arts and combat sports have a variety of methods for teaching and executing this technique. Which one is the best? The answer to this question is simple – the one which works best for you. We are all different and so each individual will favour a method that is suitable for them.

In this article I describe our approach to Mawashi Geri Gedan. This kick is devastating and can cause a lot of pain and even prevent the opponent from being able to stand or walk. Correctly executed the kick may be equivalent to being hit by a weight of up to two tonnes (metric).

We have a lot of variations of this kick. For example sometimes we kick with the foot/shin travelling upward, sometimes the kick drops down and pushes into the thigh and sometimes the kick is just a tap to score a point. All of these variations have their uses, but personally I believe that the best results are achieved when the kick is done in its most basic form where it travels along a single horizontal plane using correct body mechanics with the muscles tensing at the appropriate point.

A thigh kick is most effective and safe when

performed with the shin, as the foot is fragile. The part of the shin that comes into contact with the target is the sharp edge of the bone where there is little muscle.

When kicking this way there are two options for the setup of the foot – the toes can be pointed or the toes can be pulled up. In both cases the aim is that the foot muscles are tensed. Many injuries are caused when a kick is performed with the foot relaxed. This is because if the foot is relaxed not only are the muscles in the foot relaxed, but also the muscles in the lower part of the leg are relaxed. Kicking with the lower leg muscles relaxed can result in a broken shin.

The following description provides an overview of the basic mechanics of a thigh kick.

Let's start with the supporting leg. The correct setup of this leg is crucial to performing a powerful thigh kick (or indeed any kick). I will describe the kick from a fighting stance where our left foot is forward and the right leg will kick.

The left foot steps outward slightly (to the left) to just past the centre line of the opponent's body. When stepping the toes on the left foot turn outwards.

This move allows us to open our hips and protect our knee from over twisting. It also gives more power to the kicking leg. After moving our supporting foot we then shift our body weight to the front leg and start to lift the kicking leg up.

Our body is now ready to pivot on the support leg with the knee of the kicking leg rising to the side (we imagine that our kicking leg will have to pass over a chair that is placed right in front of the right leg). This lift gives us momentum to pivot and our kicking knee should travel in a wide arc towards the opponent, making sure that it passes the centre line of the opponent's body.

When we pivot on our supporting leg, our body has to work like a door – the left side of the body is hinged and the right side of the body can move freely about this hinge. The upper part of the body works like a counter weight and so the right arm will travel in the opposite direction to the right leg.

At the point of impact our shin hits the thigh of our opponent and at the same time our supporting knee works like a compressing spring, which makes the shin drop down further, giving us more energy. When our shin comes into contact with the thigh all of our muscles have to contract and our mind has to focus on the delivery of force to the target. Our aim is to kick just to the side of the thigh where the nerves are placed.

After kicking the right leg is pulled back quickly to avoid being caught. In our basic practice the return path is the same as the arc followed when the kick went in.

This description provides an overview of the mechanics of the kick. However, nothing can replace the feeling that is experienced when actually performing the kick, therefore it is always best to train with an instructor.

Stretching

13th of September 2014

For years I had done the traditional approach to stretching in martial arts training. This consisted of a general warm up followed by static stretching, which then moved onto kicks, punches and whatever else was being taught in the session.

Using this approach I was not able to perform high kicks for over fifteen years. I had always struggled with my suppleness and in looking for a solution to my problem lots of instructors told me that I just simply do not stretch enough. As a result I did very long sessions of stretching followed by kicking. However, I was not able to kick higher and over time I had increased pain in my muscles and joints. The effect of this was that my ability to kick actually decreased as often after sessions I had developed micro injuries and pains in my muscles that were taking a long time to heal. I had then been told by my doctor that my hips are in fact 'closed' and so I would never be able to kick high and so I dropped my strenuous stretching regime and went back to doing enough stretching to maintain mobility.

After a few months of lighter stretching I realised that I was actually able to kick higher and more freely. On discovering this I started to analyse my body's response to different forms of stretching such as dynamic, static, forced, isometric etc. From my studies came the clear view that for my body structure, the traditional methods of stretching were not suitable. Having changed my programme of stretching for a few years I can now freely kick higher than my own head height. My closed hips do not allow me to kick perfectly, but at least I know that there are other ways to improve my flexibility. Now I do five sessions of stretching a week and no longer suffer with muscle or joint pains.

Most of the martial arts training sessions that I have seen/experienced run with the same traditional model: aerobic warm up, stretching, technical then cool down. In my opinion an aspect of this cycle that is incorrect is when instructors use static stretching techniques directly after the aerobic warm up, which I believe should be used only as cool down exercises. By doing these static stretches we stretch our muscles to their maximum, which causes micro tears. This then limits our muscles' abilities to perform rapid contractions, but we then move onto dynamic techniques such as kicks. Consequently performing static stretching first can actually have a detrimental effect on our performance. As our muscles already have micro tears at this point, performing repetitive rapid contractions can cause further damage on overstretched muscles. Our trainee might not feel this damage, but with time it can accumulate and result in injury.

Our muscles respond to the micro damages in our muscle fibre by creating scarring. This scarring makes our muscles less flexible, which is why some people experience muscle tightness after intensive training and the process of stretching the muscles has to be repeated again to counteract the tightness.

In my experience it is much more efficient to use dynamic stretching as part of a warm up prior to training as this prepares our muscles to perform dynamic contractions without overstretching our muscles first. Doing dynamic instead of static stretching also helps to maintain our aerobic effort and so our body does not cool down prior to executing techniques.

For beginners we can also achieve suppleness quicker by stretching only one side of the body (unilateral) at a time. This is because when we stretch both sides of the body (bilateral) (e.g. both legs) at the same time, our nervous system responds quicker to protect our muscles from overstretching and so limits our progression. Stretching only one side at a time allows us to stretch further, but is also more representative of fighting where we only kick with one leg at a time (usually!).

All of my students are now training this way and we can all see the beneficial results, especially for those people who have been struggling with their kicks, who now love to kick to the head! As a bonus we also have not had any muscle injuries. Static stretching in our club is done only as a cool down but is used on every session.

Combining these two methods of dynamic and static stretching in this order produces better results than the more traditional setup. It is also the recommended method of stretching by experts.

I am aware that there are other methods of stretching that are effective for others as we are all different, but on the basis of my body responses over nearly 20 years, I can recommend this method as it is certainly beneficial to me and my students.

Thoughts on the Makiwara

2nd of August 2014

The makiwara is a training tool in Karate used to condition our arms and legs to create powerful blows with the unarmed weapons of our body.

There are divided opinions about the purpose of the makiwara. Some old masters say that it was just a punishment tool for misbehaving students, others that it was the most important training equipment in the dojo. My view on this is that the makiwara is a good training tool, but we cannot just rely on this kind of training. Unfortunately some Karateka overdo this type of training, which results in overgrown knuckles and body deformations.

These big knuckles may look impressive and show devotion to the art of Karate, but in reality it is an injury and is damaging to our body. Executing repetitive strikes using the knuckles helps to stimulate skin growth causing calluses to develop and cushion the knuckles, however hitting too hard causes damages to the bone in the knuckle joints. As a result of this damage the body will try to repair itself by producing new bone tissue, but this tends not to grow normally and so the new bone ends up with small pockets (a bit like pumice stone), which is similar to the effect of osteoporosis. Consequently with every harder punch parts of the new bone are crushed as the pockets collapse, leading to inflammation. Over time this may result in the movement of the hand being restricted as the fingers are prevented from completing a full range of motion. Some research also suggests a link between makiwara overtraining and arthritis, although I have not seen any conclusive evidence to support this.

Punching a rigid makiwara (i.e. one that does not flex when hit) can also cause damage to the wrists, elbows, shoulders and spine as the shock wave travels back through our body. Another unwanted reaction when punching a rigid makiwara is that it can cause whiplash - as a powerful punch is stopped suddenly, the energy of the punch is sent straight back up the arm and into the neck, similar to a car crash. Teachers often say that makiwara conditioning makes our knuckles or shins tougher or harder, but this is misconception. In order to actually achieve this we would have to repeatedly break our major bones (not the joints) and even then the bones would only become denser at the points at which they broke. What makiwara training actually does is to lower our neurological response to pain. This results in our pain barrier getting higher and so we experience less pain when punching.

Let's focus on the benefits of makiwara training where we have a properly flexible board with a nice training program including resting periods for healing and recovery. Using a makiwara enforces the proper set up of the body as when punching correctly we will feel powerful, penetrating punches. The resistance created by our equipment helps us to use accurate body positioning and mechanics. Through adjusting our stances and muscle tension we can develop a better understanding of our own body, as all of us will have different body positioning for delivering maximum power. The makiwara is perfect for giving us feedback of our body mechanics. When all of the components of a punch or kick are done well you can feel that the blow was right, on the other hand if something was out of order your body will be informed about it as the makiwara can be punishing and cause injury to your skin and joints. Through this training we learn how to be more explosive and get the most out of our body mechanics, our makiwara when it flexes mimics human soft tissues and so we learn to "push in" our strikes.

Punching our board also helps to make our joints (tendons, ligaments and muscles) stronger and more effective by overcoming the resistance and providing a shock stimulus.

I recommend makiwara training as part of the art of Karate. When first starting the use of a makiwara it is always best to do so under the instruction of a good teacher.

Sensei Makiwara – Valuable Lesson

9th of May 2015

After nearly a year of not training on a makiwara, today I decided to do a workout. I had a painful surprise as I gave it a confident, strong punch. It was very uncomfortable and a rather humbling experience.

It just goes to show that when you stop training regression kicks in and our skills diminish. This process can be translated to all skills in life.

When you stop learning you start to forget and your skills can fade. I had a very good lesson today - a big osu to my teacher, The Makiwara.

Kata Study – Tensho

23rd of June 2016

In Shin Ai Do Karate every student on one stage of their progression through grades is given a kata.

This kata is specifically chosen for your ability and character, this kata is the main one to study, you need to know other forms within the system but this one you have to specialise in and know it through throughout. For me it is Tensho kata.

I was "assigned" to study it around 15 years ago. I have tried many versions and adaptation in search of knowledge and efficacy of movement.

This kata was introduced by Chojun Miyagi in to the Goju Ryu system in 1921, as a softer Sanchin. The name Tensho is translated as "Revolving hands", "rotating palms", or "turning palms." Some researchers suggest that it is a modified version of the Rokkishu form from Chinese Kung fu.

Movements in Tensho are flowing but under tension with deep breathing, over time many versions have developed. Every master did a little bit of modification, nowadays every school where this kata is taught is thought to have their own adaptation.

In our school we teach the version introduced by Mas Oyama, although over time it has become a bit different as a few movements were changed to fit with the analysis of hands on interpretation. We are using this magnificent kata for various reasons ranging from health, strength training, self-defence, meditation, and relaxation training.

Focusing on the self-defence aspects we have three levels of understanding of Tensho:

- Kuzushi, Nage (off balancing and throwing)
- Tuite (joint manipulation)
- Atemi, Kyusho (strikes into the vital points)

Beginners are introduced to the flow of unbalancing and takedowns through the use of the stances and hands movement, alongside Tai Sabaki (body movement). In this way students learn effective ways of using their body and directions of the techniques.

An intermediate level focusses on the joint and muscle mechanics, and how to take advantage of body responses to the pain signal. All the movements are transformed to joint locks through the use of stances, the body and arms.

An advanced version exploits weak points of the body, putting pressure or strikes on to the nervous system, muscle system and other tissues of the body, causing neurological responses to the pain.

All this makes Tensho a very effective weapon in Karate, which is often not recognised and is used only as a "breathing" kata.

Performing and studying this kata for 15 years now I keep finding new ways of using it for different purposes.

Understanding this kata opens up body strength, effective self-defence and mental relaxation. Teaching it at seminars, I see more and more people are discovering the benefits of this form. Next time you do Tensho please try to find ways of applying it, and not just use it for breathing.

Balance

16th of July 2016

Working with wide a range of clients from professional athletes to office workers and from teenagers to seniors I have noticed that a significant number of them have poor balance. I have always been told that balance issues are more associated with the older generation. With time we lose our ability to move gracefully due to weakening muscles, worsening sight and the slowing down of brain function. In my work I have noticed an increasing number of young people who suffer with a lack of balance and coordination and not as a result of clinical reasons. It just seems to me that a lack of movement and physical activity is making people clumsy.

Balance, as any other skill, is fading if we do not use it, in the same way that you lose muscle strength when you do not train it. In our modern times where we spend most of the day chair bound and exercise is only done for 1 hr three times a week it is clearly not enough to keep our natural coordination and balance, which was needed by our ancestors to survive.

In the case of professional athletes the way of training is too focussed on vision instead on the quality sensory feedback from the body. In the case of multidirectional sports just relying on vision is not enough to provide enough information to the brain. If the communication centre (the brain) is not sufficiently trained in receiving and interpreting information from other parts of the body balance and coordination will be disturbed.

Lack of balance is leading to an increase in injuries for both athletes and non-athletes. You can actively fight back by doing some activities which improve your balance.

Stand on one leg

When brushing your teeth for 20 seconds or more, your brain will gather information from all of the sensors around the body and with time will learn how to process it and improve your balance. If you want to make it harder then try closing your eyes.

Take up Taiso classes

Taiso has many health and mental benefits, not just working on muscles but on the brain too and helps to calm one's mental state. Via form training we can improve strength, balance, flexibility and mobility. Our brain is stimulated by learning new patterns, building new neuron connections and reinforcing them by repetition. Natural deep breathing oxygenates blood, relaxes tension and calms the spirit.

Plyometric / Functional training

This form of training is performed with your own body weight, taking you through different variations of movement in different planes and directions. Improving strength, agility, speed and balance. From my experience this is the best way to improve overall balance in active people.

Take up dancing

It is a great and fun way of challenging your coordination and balance, going through dynamic stances your body is getting used to changes in the environment whilst at the same time improving your health.

Martial Arts

Martial arts are great for hand to eye coordination and balance as there are often changes of position and alternated use of arms and legs. Performing drills also increases the workout for the brain when memorising a sequence of moves. Along with all of the health benefits you also learn self-defence and get a boost in confidence.

Good Sleep

This is very often an overlooked aspect. Sleep deprivation will decrease brain availability to process data from our body resulting in lower balance and coordination.

Three tests to check out your balance:

1. *Both feet test*

   Stand on both feet with your ankles touching, arms across your chest and close your eyes. Ask someone to measure the time for you. It is normal to sway a little bit when you are standing with your eyes shut, you should stand for 60 seconds without moving your feet. Now test yourself by putting one foot in front of the other. You should be able to hold this position for around 40 seconds on both sides.

2. *One foot test*

   Perform this test somewhere that you can safely grab on to something, for example a door frame. Stand on one leg lifting the other without touching or resting it on the supporting leg. Close your eyes. Depending on your age you should be able to hold the pose for 30 seconds eyes open, 20 seconds with eyes closed for those who are 60 years old or younger. People aged 61 and older: 22 seconds with eyes open, 10 seconds with eyes closed.

3. *Ball of the foot test*

Stand on one foot with your hands on your hips and place the non-supporting foot against the inside knee of the standing leg. Raise your heel off floor and hold the pose—you should be able to do so for 25 seconds.

Seiza "Proper Sitting"

23rd of December 2016

Throughout the early history of Japan various ways of sitting were regarded as 'proper', such as sitting cross-legged, sitting with one knee raised, or sitting to the side. People's social circumstances, clothing styles, and the places where they sat naturally brought about their manners of sitting. The development in the Muromachi period of Japanese architecture in which the floors were completely covered with tatami (thick straw mats), combined with the strict formalities of the ruling warrior class for which this style of architecture was principally designed, heralded the adoption of the sitting posture known today as seiza as the respectful way to sit. However, it probably was not until circa the turn of the 18th century (the Genroku to Kyōhō eras in Japanese history) that the Japanese generally adopted this manner of sitting in their everyday lives. By the end of the 20th century the traditional tatami-floored rooms and the circumstances where one should sit 'properly' on a tatami had become uncommon in Japan. Consequently, many modern-day Japanese are unaccustomed to sitting in seiza.[11]

Performing seiza is an integral and required part of several traditional Japanese arts, such as certain martial

---

[11] Japanese online Encyclopaedia of Japanese Culture (http://iroha-japan.net/iroha/B06_custom/03_seiza.html)

arts and the tea ceremony (a table-style version of the tea ceremony known as ryūrei was invented in the 19th century). Seiza is also the traditional way of sitting while doing arts such as shodo (calligraphy) and ikebana (flower arranging), though with the increasing use of western-style furniture it is not always necessary nowadays.

Many theatres for traditional performing arts such as kabuki and sumo still have audience seating sections where the spectators sit in seiza.

Use in the Karate Dojo

Seiza sitting is a posture used in the dojo for Zazen (seated meditation). The body weight is distributed over the knees and buttocks whilst the spine is in a neutral position. In Shin Ai Do Karate we keep our hands open on the thighs. Open hands symbolise non aggressiveness. Elbows are placed close to the body. The right instep is crossed over the left instep. The shoulders are held slightly back and relaxed. The chin is tucked in with the body elongated.

Spine in Seiza

The major points to note in sitting in this position are weight distribution and alignment of the body. The most stable position is created by three points of support in seiza. These points are our knees and buttocks resting on our feet. Once we have found a stable position we need to find the optimal alignment for the spine.

Many Sensei teach that students should sit with the back straight, but this action causes tension and quick tiredness. It is nearly impossible to hold yourself like this for long periods of time.

To maximise the benefits of performing seiza our spine should strive to be relaxed and elongated, avoiding compression. The spine will be naturally curved and the pelvis should be tilted slightly forward. These two actions help the vertebra align in a proper position (assuming the practitioner has no health issues). The stomach will not become compressed and we can breathe freely. The chin should be tucked in and pushed back imaging that we have a balloon attached to the head stretching us up.

Problems with Seiza

Some beginners might have problems with this position as it demands good flexibility in the knees and hips. Some might experience tiredness in the back as they are not used to sitting straight (as a result of long periods of slouching). Many people hold tension in the neck and shoulders, they might find it difficult to relax in seiza. Others with weak back muscles might experience slumping in the hips and an arching back. Students with hip mobility restrictions may prefer one hip to the other, which can cause instability. Many students have mobility problems in the knees and ankles.

Overcoming Problems

With all the techniques in Karate you need patience. It is the same with seiza. Give yourself time to master it. Be aware of the problems every time you sit and try to use the correct form. We are looking for a balanced posture. Our European bad habits of sitting may make the task of perfecting seiza take a bit longer, but with practice comes mastery.

From Kata to Fighting

12th of July 2019

Kata (form) – Karate shadow boxing. The mention of Kata evokes all sorts of emotions in people. From passion to laughter everyone has an opinion ranging from a functional self defence training tool to merely a comical dance performed by kids in pyjamas. Unfortunately over the years this picture of a dance has been painted by an ignorance of Karate teachers. This has led to the display of unrealistic applications for the moves within the forms with a total disregard for anatomy, physiology and common sense. As a result we see demonstrations of techniques out of this world which have no real chance of working.

Kata is an essential part of Karate. Most masters agree that the pure essence of Karate are its forms, but forms that are understood and studied not just copied and mindlessly repeated.

"Like textbooks to a student or tactical exercises to a solider, kata are the most important element of Karate." Gichin Funakoshi

"In Karate, the most important thing is kata. Into the kata of Karate are woven every manner of attack and defence technique. Therefore, kata must be practiced properly, with a good understanding of their bunkai meaning." Kenwa Mabuni

For me kata must be functional, not necessarily looking very crisp with structured timings. The latter attributes are great for sport competition and aesthetics, but when I look at that type of performance I can see that often performers don't know why they do all of the moves within the given form. It is a very athletic and eye pleasing performance but function is left behind.

"Never be shackled by the rituals of kata but instead move freely according to the opponent's strengths and weaknesses." Nakasone

I value more a kata where I can see that the person executing it knows why he does what he does. The movement may not be so precise but it screams that I'm doing 'this' now.

"We must be careful to not overlook the fact that kata, and the body positions that comprises them, are just templates of sort; it is their application in combat which needs to be mastered." Choki Motobu

At my club beginners don't start with learning the form pattern, they are introduced to the principles and partner work alongside the kata. In my experience it is easier for students to learn a form if they understand what they are doing.

When students grasp the basic concepts then we can focus on technical aspects of a kata and polishing technique. The next step is to introduce partner work with little resistance, so the practitioner can find the right technical pathway to make a technique work. When this is achieved we add another layer whereby the compliance is decreased, but trainees are sticking to the structure of one attack one defence. In this way they have a basis of understanding ingrained for an application of an element of a kata and they can follow closely the kata's path.

Evolving on from a low level of resistance we move on to pressure testing where a student will still stay with a given application but wears protective gear and resistance is applied. There is no continuity after the initial attack, students focus on one given attribute and try to make it work under pressure. The next step is full interaction with a live resisting opponent who is allowed to fight back. The "defender" at this stage is still trying to make the chosen application work. The last stage of this learning is a free work where one partner is the attacker and the other is defender. The defender has the kata available to use and can use freely parts of the form depending on the need in the moment. For example he can choose to start with an opening section moving on to the last part of the kata as circumstances change and follow that with the middle part of the form if necessary.

The final stage is sparring – not the sport style of sparring but starting from a dispute and then one partner decides to attack. The defenders target is to fight back and try to use the kata's tools to achieve an opportunity to escape or disable the opponent's ability or will to attack. In this stage we don't worry about which kata part is used or joined together if it's effective.

Forgotten Recovery

28th of June 2014

How many times have you heard from your teachers, friends or fitness people the phrases *"do more", "try harder", "no pain no gain"* etc.? These are all very challenging words that are aimed at pushing you that little bit further in your physical and mental progression, but how often do you hear phrases such as *"stop, have a rest", "you should take a break", "you need to recover"*?

We all like to think that training to the maximum limits is the best way even though working out smarter is much healthier for our mind and body than working out harder.

It is common knowledge that the body needs time to recover, but we rarely hear about resting our nervous system, not to mention our psychological wellbeing. Overloading our systems is no good: too much stimulation pushes us into regression.

This issue of lack of emphasis on recovery has led me to do some research into how we can be more efficient in training. The following information I have gleaned from reading such books as:

- *"Strength training anatomy"* by Frederic Delavier; Michael Gundill (2005), Human Kinetics Publishers

173

- *"Periodization Training for Sports"* by Tudor Bompa; Michael Carrera (2005), Human Kinetics Publishers

For those who are interested in finding out more about recovery, I would highly recommend the above two books.

So let's start by looking at different types of recovery. We have five types of recovery system:

- Energy recovery
- Hormone recovery
- Contractile system recovery
- Joint and tendon recovery
- Nervous system recovery

All of these systems in themselves will need time to recover. The length of time required for regeneration depends upon the intensity of the workout and the technique(s) used. All of us have our own unique recovery times. The systems mentioned above differ in their "recharging" rate, not only because of the amount of time they need but also because they recover via different mechanisms.

- Energy recovery – after working out our energy level is low and it should be topped up by nutrition and supplements. If our nutrition intake is adequate our energy recovery should be completed in a few hours.

- Hormone recovery – our hormone balance changes after an intense workout. Our overall testosterone level will fall and cortisol levels will rise. This distortion should pass after 24-48 hours after an intense workout. When completing workouts back to back with similar intensity the changes in our hormones will increase further as the body does not have time to recover to normal levels in between. This is why it is recommended that people have a day or two to rest between similar workouts.

- Contractile system – the recovery of small muscles after moderate workout takes around 16 hours, with larger muscles taking around 24 to 48 hours to recover, and so we can see that different parts of the body will recover at different rates.

- Joint and tendon recovery – our joints during a heavy workout are put under a lot stress. If we do not allow adequate time for recovery, over time we will slowly develop chronic pain and may experience limitations in movement and the loss of ability to do certain exercises. We have to be especially careful with larger joints as they are used in multiple exercises, for example the shoulders and hips.

- Nervous system recovery – when training our brain sends signal to our muscles through a network of nerves. Just like our muscles, our nervous system will get fatigued, which will result in the signals getting slower and weaker. The recovery of the nervous system is very slow. A study was published in the Journal of the Neurological Science[12] which showed that recovery following a heavy thigh workout resulted in:

1. Muscle soreness, which lasted for 5 days
2. Loss of strength for 7 days
3. Distortion of the nervous system for more than 10 days

Another system which needs recovery is our psychological system. If we continuously workout without rest our body and brain becomes exhausted, which can lead to monotony and a lack of motivation that can stop our progression. In the same way that we need to take holidays away from work, we need to take breaks from our sport/art. If we take regular breaks from our workout routine to recovery our body and mind then after that break we will regain a feeling of hunger for training and when we start working out again we will progress. The required length and frequency of these breaks will depend on the individual. Some people will be refreshed after a couple of days, others after a couple

---

[12] Deschenes, M R et al., Neuromuscular disturbance outlasts other symptoms of exercise-induced muscle damage, 2000, Journal of the Neurological Sciences (Volume 174, Issue 2)

of weeks. Some people will want to take a yearly break from their training whilst others may have to take a break from their workouts once a month or once a week.

When resting all of our recovery systems this does not mean that we should just sit and do nothing. Studies have shown that active rest speeds up recovery times in comparison to non-active. That is why it is a good idea to engage in other light sports or activities when resting to stimulate other nerves paths and let the weary circuits have a deserved rest.

I hope that the next time someone says *"no pain no gain", "do more",* or *"be tough"* we will also consider the possibility of doing smarter workouts and ensuring that we include resting as a part of our training regime...

Chapter 6 - Summary

If you have got to this part of the book I salute you, you have survived my rambling about Karate and related topics. I hope that some of the material in this collection was thought provoking, regardless of whether or not you agree or disagree with my point of view. I'm very thankful for your time and hope that you have your own opinion on the subject. Karate needs people who can think for themselves not those that are blindly following their teachers. We as a community of martial artists need to modify and make Karate better. Incorporating new methods of training based on science, and adapting Karate to the needs of society. Each of us might use Karate for different purposes and that is great, I always refer to the many faces of Karate. We can all find the right use for our needs.

This collection of articles contains my past and current thoughts on Karate, in the future I might change my mind about certain things depending on my personal experiences and the facts presented to me. If you would like to discuss any of the articles or have views that you would like to share on the subjects covered here, please feel free to get in touch via email at info@lesbubka.co.uk.

Once again thank you for your time and support.

Warm wishes,

Les Bubka

One more thing. To fully understand my way of modifying Karate is to know my background and my fight with anxiety, for that I recommend my biography book, Anxious Black Belt, which contains detailed information about my road to recovery.

About the Author

Les Bubka is a dedicated practitioner of the way of the empty hand and has been for over twenty years. He is the founder of Les Bubka Karate Jutsu, which incorporates the art of Karate with his personal training qualifications in order to help people.

Les has experience in running projects in association with mental health charities and other institutions, introducing Karate as a tool to help build confidence, self-esteem and physical activity to disadvantaged members of the community.

Les runs an inclusive club in Guildford (UK) where everyone is welcome.

Les is an established author, with his first book, Anxious Black Belt, being well received within the martial arts community.

For more information about Les Bubka and to connect with him directly please visit:

www.lesbubka.co.uk

Printed in Great Britain
by Amazon